amazing
iceddesserts

amazing
iceddesserts

irresistible frozen creations from sumptuous gâteaux to simple sorbets

joanna farrow

southwater

This edition is published by Southwater

Distributed in the UK by
The Manning Partnership
251–253 London Road East
Batheaston
Bath BA1 7RL
tel. 01225 852 727
fax 01225 852 852

Published in the USA by
Anness Publishing Inc.
27 West 20th Street
Suite 504
New York NY 10011
fax 212 807 6813

Distributed in Canada by
General Publishing
895 Don Mills Road
400–2 Park Centre
Toronto, Ontario M3C 1W3
tel. 416 445 3333
fax 416 445 5991

Distributed in Australia by
Sandstone Publishing
Unit 1, 360 Norton Street
Leichhardt
New South Wales 2040
tel. 02 9560 7888
fax 02 9560 7488

Southwater is an imprint of Anness Publishing Limited
Hermes House 88–89 Blackfriars Road London SE1 8HA
tel. 020 7401 2077 fax 020 7633 9499

© Anness Publishing Limited 2001

10 9 8 7 6 5 4 3 2 1

PUBLISHER: Joanna Lorenz
MANAGING EDITOR: Linda Fraser
SENIOR EDITOR: Margaret Malone
DESIGNER: Luise Roberts
PHOTOGRAPHY: Gus Filgate (recipes) and Craig Robertson
FOOD FOR PHOTOGRAPHY: Joanna Farrow (recipes), Annabel Ford
(equipment, techniques, and steps)
STYLING: Penny Markham
EDITORIAL READER: Joy Wotton

Previously published as part of a larger compendium,
Ice Cream and Iced Desserts

NOTES
Bracketed terms are intended for American readers. For all
recipes, quantities are given in both metric and imperial
measures and, where appropriate, measures are also
given in standard cups and spoons. Follow one set,
but not a mixture because they are not interchangeable.
Standard spoon and cup measures are level.
1 tsp = 5ml, 1 tbsp = 15ml, 1 cup = 250ml/8fl oz
Australian standard tablespoons are 20ml.
Australian readers should use 3 tsp in place of 1 tbsp for measuring small quantities
of gelatine, flour, salt etc. Medium (US large) eggs are used unless otherwise stated.

contents

Introduction **6**

Essential Equipment **8**

Basic Ingredients **10**

Preparing Ice Cream **12**

Preparing Water Ices **14**

Baskets and Biscuits **16**

Toppings and Decorations **19**

bombes & terrines 22

tortes & gâteaux 36

hot ice cream desserts 52

elegant iced desserts 66

ice creams with fruit 86

herb, spice & flower ices 98

iced drinks 114

Introduction **126**

Introduction

Ice cream must be one of the few dishes in the world that is loved by virtually everyone, from the young to the young at heart, from the out-and-out foodie, searching for the ultimate flavour combination, to the devotee with more traditional tastes and a preference for timeless and classic favourites.

AN ADAPTABLE TREAT

With ice cream, there really is something for everyone. At one end of the spectrum is the simple ice cream cone – quite irresistible on a hot summer's day – while at the other is the elaborate layered mould, perfect for entertaining. In between come the lighter ices, including refreshing fruit sorbets (sherbets) and snow-like granitas, ideal for serving between courses to cleanse the palate, after an elegant supper or relaxed *al fresco* meal.

Within this wonderful recipe collection are the very best tortes, gâteaux and bombes, plus beautiful fruit, herb, spice and flower iced desserts. Recipes range from stunning but surprisingly easy creations to the impressively elaborate. You'll find classic iced desserts, such as Caramel and Pecan Terrine and Cassata, plus more adventurous mixtures that prove just how exciting working with ice cream can be. There are also tempting hot iced desserts and delicious iced drinks.

DESSERTS FOR EVERY OCCASION

The recipes in this book are divided into seven chapters, ranging from the simple to the sublime. The first two chapters will delight all those who like to end a meal in style; bombes and terrines and tortes and gâteaux contain stunning iced desserts that utilize simple, but effective techniques such as marbling, layering, speckling with fruit and nuts and encasing in sponge, meringue or crisp biscuit. These desserts are full of flavour, texture and colour – for example try Rippled Nectarine and Muscovado Terrine, Pistachio and Nougat Torte and Chocolate, Rum and Raisin Roulade for a sophisticated finish to a meal.

The next chapter, hot ice cream desserts, is truly decadent, with soft, melting ice cream centres combined with warm pastry, hot sauces or warm fruit compotes. Coconut and Passion Fruit Alaskas

ABOVE: *Made with simple ingredients, sorbet (sherbet) is a light and tasty dessert.*

and Orange Crêpes with Mascarpone Cream are just two superb examples. These are puddings and desserts just made for cold winter evenings or an indulgent breakfast.

For the clever entertainer, elegant iced desserts contains ideas for iced creations that look stunning but are extremely easy to assemble. The key to these desserts is fantastic presentation. Chocolate cases, ice bowls, biscuits and cones transform simple ice cream into beautiful desserts. There are even ideas for using nature's own cases, such as Coconut Ice Cream with Mango Sauce.

Ice cream with fruit, herbs, spices or flowers is a classic combination. Marrying colour, flavour, texture and aroma, the recipes in these two chapters will provide the perfect finale on a warm summer's day or to a rich meal. Some of these recipes are frozen versions of well-known desserts, such as Iced Summer Pudding, while others explore new flavours, such as Lavender and Honey Ice Cream and tangy Basil and Orange Granita.

The last chapter contains iced drinks that just burst with colour and fizz. Almost a drink and a dessert in one, there are all the favourite classic drinks such as Iced Margaritas, Sparkling Peach Melba and Strawberry Daiquiri.

PROFESSIONAL TIPS

There are lots of helpful tips for making successful ices with or without an ice cream maker, and advice on the best way to store iced desserts after you have made them. Throughout the book, detailed serving instructions give guidance on transforming simple scoops of ice cream or sorbet into desserts that would not look out of place in the smartest restaurant. A handy techniques section at the beginning of the book covers all you need to know to improvise and use moulds, how to make your own baskets, biscuits and cones, and there are also some wonderful topping and decoration ideas.

ABOVE: *Though it looks impressive, Chocolate, Rum and Raisin Roulade can be frozen a week in advance for easy entertaining.*

AN INTERNATIONAL FLAVOUR

From humble beginnings, ice cream and ices have evolved into truly sophisticated creations, found the world over, and the recipes in this book reflect this diversity. The range of recipes includes ice creams and water ices from Eastern Europe, the British Isles, the Mediterranean, India and the Americas. Many of these are familiar mixtures, but some are sweetened with honey or maple syrup instead of sugar, while others are based upon yogurt or boiled milk, rather than cream. Some of the more unusual flavourings include flower essences, herbs (such as lavender and bay), nuts and even spices.

ABOVE: *Ice Cream Croissants with Chocolate Sauce make an irresistibly easy breakfast treat.*

For those who wish to impress their friends with their culinary skill, the recipe section includes elaborate moulded desserts and terrines, extravagant bombes and mousses and a wide selection of sophisticated and elegant desserts. These ices look sensational, and most of the effects are surprisingly easy to achieve. Iced gâteaux, for instance, come in all sorts of shapes and guises. There are also plenty of ideas for using ice cream with fruit and nut, biscuit and meringue – the combinations are endless and the results outstanding. Strawberry ice cream and lemon curd or rich chocolate ice cream and brownies complement each other perfectly. The more unusual iced brûlées, roulades or tortes look and taste superb, while ice cream sundaes get a modern makeover when layered in elegant glasses with fruit and liqueur sauces. For an element of surprise, impress your friends and families with hot ices. Try individual Baby Alaskas, little meringue mountains containing a delicious centre of liqueur-flavoured apricots, or Apple Ice Cream with Cinnamon Bread – a delicious way to use up extra apples.

ABOVE: *This delicate Walnut Castle is a delightful adaptation of traditional Indian kulfi; ideal for a summer treat.*

In this modern age, when electrical equipment is readily available, it is easy to forget that there was ever a time without the domestic freezer. Yet 300 years ago, when ice cream was becoming popular in Europe as the ultimate dessert for the very rich, the only way to freeze it in summer was by using ice which was cut from frozen lakes in winter and stored in deep underground pits. Imagine the dazzling spectacle it must have made when served at large dinners or a ball.

Ice cream is no longer a symbol of wealth, but is one of life's affordable luxuries. Universally acknowledged as one of the best loved comfort foods, it gives you a lift when you need it, and many problems have been solved – or friendships forged – over a shared tub of luxurious chocolate ripple or rocky road. Of course, ice cream can be mass-produced, with cheaper ingredients than any you'll find in this book, but there is really no substitute for the real thing in all its flavour-filled glory.

Essential equipment

You will probably already have most of the equipment you need to make successful ice creams and water ices. Ices made by hand can simply be frozen in a plastic tub or box in the freezer, although very keen ice cream enthusiasts may want to invest in a free-standing electric machine.

BASIC EQUIPMENT FOR MAKING ICES

Making ices by hand is the simplest method of all, and is known as "still freezing". All that you need are glass bowls and a fork, a manual or electric hand-held whisk for beating and a freezerproof container with a lid. You will also need a heavy pan for making the custard, sugar syrups and cooking fruits, plus a sieve for puréeing and a lemon squeezer and fine grater for citrus fruits.

A food processor is a useful aid for breaking down the ice crystals, although it can be wasteful of ingredients; however, this labour-saving method does produce a similar texture to that made in an electric ice cream maker.

For storage

You will need a selection of freezerproof containers in varying sizes, with tight-fitting lids to eliminate the transfer of strong smells and flavours and prevent the surface of the ice cream from drying out. Use containers a little larger than the quantity of ice cream, to allow for beating during freezing and increased volume when frozen. A headspace of 2cm|¾in is adequate. Granita, however, requires as shallow a container as possible to reduce freezing time. Only use stainless steel or aluminium while making ice cream or sorbet (sherbet) as other metals can impart a metallic taste.

The freezer

An upright or chest domestic freezer is the essential item of equipment. For making ice cream the temperature should be -18°C|-66°F. A freezer thermometer is a very useful tool. The colder the freezer the more quickly the ice will freeze, making smaller ice crystals and smoother ice cream. If the freezer is badly packed, the motor will have to work harder to maintain temperature.

Adding volume

1 Using a fork requires more effort, but is an effective way of increasing volume by introducing air into sorbet and granitas.

For making parfait

You will need a good sugar thermometer for these; a parfait is made by whisking a hot sugar syrup into beaten egg yolks, and the correct temperature ensures perfect results. Choose one with a clip to hold it in place on the pan.

For making moulded iced desserts

Specialist equipment is available, but you can usually improvise with bowls from your kitchen.

2 For making large quantities of ice cream, a hand-held electric whisk saves time and adds even more volume to the mixture.

ICE CREAM MAKERS

These labour-saving electric machines vary greatly in price. The two basic types are those with a built-in freezing unit and those with a detachable double-skinned bowl which has to be pre-frozen before use. There are also ice cream machines that can be run inside a standard freezer. These have very poor motors and similar, if not better, results can be obtained by making ice cream by hand.

The most efficient – and most expensive – models are those with an integral freezing unit. Motors vary, depending on the make of the machine. If you are investing in an ice cream maker, choose the one with the most powerful motor and if possible see it in operation, as noise levels vary considerably. As this type of ice cream maker tends to be larger than a food processor, working and storage space are prime considerations. These machines come with two bowls, a stainless-steel bowl built into the unit and a separate aluminium bucket that can be slotted into the larger fixed bowl. Most machines of this type have a see-through lid for easy viewing, plus a vent for pouring in additional ingredients. This plastic top simply slides off for easy washing.

RIGHT: *Ice cream maker with integral motor and freezing unit.*

Pre-freezing ice cream maker

For a slightly cheaper option, look out for a model with a detachable double-skinned bowl filled with freezing liquid. This type of machine requires the bowl to be frozen for at least 18 hours before use. When you are ready to use the ice cream maker, you simply fit the motor and paddle to the frozen bowl, switch on the power, and fill the bowl with the ice cream or sorbet mixture. It usually takes 25–40 minutes for the ice cream to churn.

If the freezer is large enough, the bowl can be stored there, giving the option to make home-made ice cream at any time. For larger quantities, it is very useful to have a second detachable bowl on standby and make two batches of ice cream.

ABOVE: *Simple ice cream maker with motorized paddles.*

UNMOULDING AN ICED DESSERT

An easy way of removing an iced pudding from its mould is to invert it on the serving plate and cover the mould with a clean dish towel that has been dipped in boiling water and then wrung out. Leave the dish towel in place for a few seconds, and lift off the mould. Another option is to dip the mould itself into hot water. This is a good method when using small individual moulds.

1 Dip the filled metal or plastic mould into hot water and leave it for a couple of seconds. Lift it out and blot the excess water. If the mould is lined with clear film, carefully insert a knife between the film and the mould to loosen the ice cream.

Freezing ice cream

Beating or churning

Freezing is obviously a crucial stage in the making of a home-made ice cream, and there are two basic methods. Freezing without a machine is also known as "still freezing", while the action in an ice cream maker is "stir freezing". We are so used to electrical machines that it is hard to envisage how labour-intensive the process must have been for the cooks of one hundred years ago beating ice cream by hand in churns stood in packed ice hewn from frozen lakes. Making ice cream by hand today requires freezing it in a tub or similar container

Freezing with an ice cream maker

1 Having prepared your ice cream maker according to the manufacturer's instructions, pour the chilled custard and whipping cream into the bowl, fit the paddle, secure the lid and begin churning.

2 After 10–15 minutes of churning, the ice cream will have begun to freeze. The mixture will thicken and will start to look slushy. Continue to churn the mixture in the same way.

2 Invert the dessert on a serving plate, lift off the mould and peel away the clear film. If you have difficulty turning out the dessert, repeat the process as before.

and beating it several times during the freezing process. It is this beating or churning process that is done automatically in an ice cream maker.

The secret of a really good ice cream is the formation of minute ice crystals. The finished ice cream should be light and taste cold, not icy. If the ice crystals are large, the ice cream will have a grainy, coarse texture, which will detract from the creamy, smooth taste you are aiming to achieve. Beating the ice cream, either by hand or with an ice cream maker, breaks down the crystals. The more it is beaten while it is freezing, the finer the finished texture will be.

3 After 20–25 minutes, the ice cream will be considerably thicker. It will still be too soft to scoop, but this is the ideal stage to mix in your chosen additional flavourings, such as praline or browned breadcrumbs.

Basic ingredients

Nothing beats the cool, creamy smoothness of the ultimate indulgence, home-made ice cream. The choice of flavours and taste combinations is limited only by your own imagination, so begin with our basic formulae and adapt or develop them to incorporate all the tastes you love. You will rapidly build a repertoire of wonderful iced desserts, all completely additive-free and made with only the ingredients that you choose to be there.

Ice cream

Cream

You just couldn't make true ice cream without lashings of cream. Surprisingly, whipping cream, with its natural creamy taste, makes the best ice cream, especially when mixed with strong rich flavours such as coffee, toffee or chocolate. Double (heavy) cream is, however, a must for vanilla or brown bread ice cream. Clotted cream and crème fraîche, the thick, rich lightly soured French-style cream, make delicious additions to fruit, honey and spice ice creams. Do be careful when using double or clotted cream as their high butterfat content can give the ice cream a buttery flavour and texture, especially if it is overchurned. Avoid UHT creams as the flavour is so obvious and strong.

ABOVE: *New-laid eggs and double or whipping cream give home-made ice cream its luxury flavour.*

Milk

There is a wide choice of milks in most supermarkets, from skimmed, semi-skimmed (low-fat), full-fat (whole) and breakfast milk to the now more readily available goat's milk and soya milk. Skimmed milk is best avoided when making ice cream at home, due to its low fat content and "thin" taste, but it is difficult to distinguish between semi-skimmed or full-fat milk, especially when they are mixed with cream. Full fat, semi-skimmed and goat's milk all make delicious ice cream.

Yogurt

The choice of yogurt is highly personal: it seems people either love ice cream that contains yogurt or absolutely hate it! If you are not sure how your family will react, start with the mild bio-style natural (plain) yogurt, with its creamy smoothness, and, if that is successful, work up to the stronger, sharper sheep's and goat's milk yogurts.

Cheeses

Light, virtually fat-free fromage frais can be added to fruit or vanilla ice creams and is ideal for those who adore ice cream but have to watch their fat intake. Ricotta, an Italian whey cheese, has a white, creamy, soft texture. It is rather like a cross between cottage and cream cheese and can be used successfully in certain ice creams. For the richest results of all, try mascarpone, another Italian cheese. It has a deep-buttery yellow colour and a texture similar to that of cream cheese. For the best of both worlds, mix mascarpone with fromage frais for a rich tasting, fat-reduced dessert.

Non-dairy products

Look out for soya milk, either unsweetened or sweetened, in longlife cartons, and canned coconut milk – both ideal for vegans or those on a milk-free diet. Coconut milk is also a great standby for a dinner party ice cream when mixed with lime or lemon.

Eggs

Where possible use new-laid, organic eggs for the best colour and flavour. They cost very little more than ordinary eggs but do make such a difference to the finished result of home-made ice cream.

ABOVE: *Muscovado sugar can be a delicious sweetener.*

Sweeteners

Caster (superfine) sugar has been used in most recipes, as its fine crystals dissolve quickly in the custard, maintaining a smooth, silky texture. Granulated sugar is used for making praline, a delicious ingredient in some of the speciality ices. Light brown and dark brown muscovado (molasses) sugar can also be used as a sweetener, where the darker colour and stronger flavour work to great effect. Honey and maple syrup also make delicious additions, either on their own or mixed with caster sugar. They are particularly good in ice cream flavoured with nuts.

Cornflour

Many purists will throw their hands up in horror at the idea of cornflour (cornstarch) being used in the custard for an ice cream. They might well argue that it is far better to make the custard in a double boiler or a large heatproof bowl set over simmering water. It is certainly true that cornflour is not a standard ingredient in a classic custard, but it does help to stabilize the custard and reduces the risk of curdling. Custard which contains a little cornflour is easier to handle, so it can be gently cooked in a heavy pan. It will thicken in 4–5 minutes as against 15 minutes or more in a double boiler, greatly reducing the cooking time.

COOK'S TIP *Put leftover egg whites in a small plastic box. Cover with a tight-fitting lid and label the box clearly. Freeze up to 6 months and thaw at room temperature for 4 hours. Use to make pavlovas, meringues and meringue-based ice creams.*

Water ices

Sugar syrup

A simple sugar syrup is made by heating a mixture of caster sugar and water in a medium saucepan, stirring until the sugar has dissolved. It is no longer thought essential to boil the syrup, just to heat it for long enough to dissolve the sugar. Caster sugar has been used for syrups in the recipe section of this book because it dissolves very rapidly, but granulated sugar can also be used, as can light brown sugar or honey. Once made and cooled, the syrup can be stored in the refrigerator for several days.

Flavouring

Choose from a wide range of fresh fruit purées such as strawberry, raspberry, peach or pineapple, or mix with some of the more exotic fruits such as passion fruit, mango and lime. Dried fruits are sometimes steeped in apple or grape juice or in water and brandy or a liqueur mixture before being puréed. Citrus rinds (orange, lemon or lime) can be infused in the hot syrup for extra flavour and then fresh juice added to heighten and strengthen the flavour. Spice infusions or mixtures of spices and fruits also work very well and create unusual ices that are particularly successful with those who prefer a light dessert that is not too sweet.

ABOVE: *Honey can be used on its own or with sugar.*

Egg white

The purpose of adding egg white to a semi-frozen sorbet (sherbet) is twofold. Firstly, it stabilizes the mixture, which is important for those sorbets that melt quickly, and secondly, it can be used to lighten very dense or fibrous sorbets such as those made from blackcurrants or blackberries. The egg white requires only the minimum beating with a fork to loosen it and need not be beaten until frothy or standing in peaks as used to be suggested.

HOW TO SEPARATE AN EGG

Crack the egg on the side of a bowl. Gently ease the halves apart, keeping the yolk in one half and letting the white fall into the bowl below. Separate any remaining egg white from the yolk by swapping the yolk from one shell half to the other. Do this several times if necessary, until all the egg white has fallen into the bowl and what remains is the pure egg yolk. If you do drop any egg yolk into the bowl below, scoop it out with one of the eggshell halves; the jagged edges will trap the yolk and prevent it from sliding back into the bowl.

Preparing ice cream

Many classic ice creams are based on a custard made from eggs and milk. It is not difficult to make, but as it is used so frequently, it is worth perfecting the technique by following these very simple guidelines.

How to make a classic ice cream

Making the custard base

INGREDIENTS

FLAVOURING to INFUSE (optional)

300ml | ½ pint | 1¼ cups
SEMI-SKIMMED (LOW-FAT) MILK

4 EGG YOLKS

75g | 3oz | 6 tbsp CASTER (SUPERFINE) SUGAR

5ml | 1 tsp CORNFLOUR (CORNSTARCH)

BATCH COOKING

If you are planning to make ice cream for a party, make double quantities of custard to save time. It is not advisable, however, to increase the quantities any more than this or it would be difficult to heat the custard evenly. It is quicker and easier to make up two double-quantity batches in separate pans and a lot safer than running the risk of curdling one pan of custard made with a dozen eggs!

1 Prepare any flavourings. Split vanilla pods (beans) with a sharp knife; crack coffee beans with a mallet. Cinnamon sticks, whole cloves, fresh rosemary and lavender sprigs or bay leaves can be used as they are.

2 Pour the milk into a pan. Bring to the boil, then remove the pan from the heat, add the chosen flavouring and leave to infuse for 30 minutes or until cool.

3 If you have used a vanilla pod, lift it out of the pan, and scrape the seeds back into the milk to enrich the flavour. Whisk the egg yolks, caster sugar and cornflour in a bowl until thick and foamy. Bring the plain or infused milk to the boil, then gradually whisk it into the yolk mixture. Pour the combined mixture back into the pan.

4 Cook the mixture over a low heat, stirring it continuously until it approaches boiling point and thickens to a consistency where the custard will coat the back of a wooden spoon. Do not let the custard overheat or it may curdle. Take the pan off the heat and continue stirring, making sure you take the spoon right around the bottom edges of the pan.

5 Pour the custard into a bowl and cover the surface with clear film (plastic wrap) to prevent the formation of a skin, or cover the surface with a light sprinkling of caster sugar. Leave to cool, then chill until required. If you are making the ice cream in a machine, ensure the custard is chilled before starting.

COOK'S TIP *Reduce the temperature of custard by pouring it into a cool bowl. Stand this in a larger bowl of cold or iced water and change the water as it warms.*

RESCUING CURDLED CUSTARD

Quickly take the pan off the heat and plunge it into a sink or a roasting pan, half filled with cold water. Stir the custard frequently, taking the spoon right into the bottom edges of the pan. Keep stirring for 4–5 minutes until the temperature of the custard has dropped and the custard has stabilized. It may also be helpful to whisk the mixture. If all else fails, strain it through a sieve.

Using flavourings

If you haven't infused the milk, you may wish to flavour the custard. For chocolate custard, break white, dark (bittersweet) or milk chocolate into pieces and stir these into the hot custard in the pan, off the heat. Stir occasionally for 5 minutes until the chocolate has melted completely, then pour into a bowl, cover and cool. Chill in the refrigerator.

Other flavourings that can be added include strong coffee (either filter or instant dissolved in boiling water), flower waters (such as orange flower water or rose water) and sweeteners that also add flavour, such as maple syrup or honey. Vanilla, peppermint or almond essence (extract) are popular flavourings. These should be added to the custard when cool.

THE TASTE TEST

If you like to be imaginative and invent your own flavour combinations for ice cream, taste the mixture before freezing. Aim for a taste that is a little stronger or sweeter than you would like the finished dessert to be as the formation of ice crystals will slightly dilute the flavour of the finished ice cream. There is no limit to the combinations that can be tried, and ice cream making is a perfect means of expression for the creative cook. Flavour combinations that work well with other dishes will often adapt to ice creams but always remember to taste the result.

FRUIT AND CREAM COMBINATIONS

Although you can make delicious fruit ice creams with a custard base, the combination of custard, cream and fruit purée can sometimes be too rich and dull the fresh fruit flavour, robbing it of its intensity. Many cooks prefer to omit the custard base and simply use sieved fresh berry fruit, simple purées or lightly poached and puréed orchard fruits stirred into whipped cream.

If you are making a fruit ice cream in an ice cream maker, you can speed up the churning time by partially freezing the purée before stirring in the cream.

Adding cream

If you are making ice cream in an ice cream maker, follow the preliminary instructions for your specific machine, pre-cooling the machine or chilling the bowl in the freezer. Stir whipping cream, whipped double (heavy) cream or any soft cream cheeses into the chilled plain or flavoured custard and churn until firm.

Creams with a high fat proportion – double cream, clotted cream or crème fraîche – should only be added to ice creams that are partially frozen, as they have a tendency to become buttery if churned for too long. Double cream is sometimes added at the start, but only for small quantities and minimal churning times.

Make the ice cream by hand in a freezerproof container, by folding soft whipped cream into the chilled plain or flavoured custard and pouring the mixture into the tub. Allow enough space for beating the ice cream during freezing. Crème fraîche, clotted cream and cream cheeses can also be added at this stage.

Preparing water ices

Sorbets or sherbets, like water ices, are made with a light sugar syrup flavoured with fruit juice, fruit purée, wine, liqueur, tea or herbs. They should not contain milk or cream, and are best made in an ice cream maker, as the constant churning ensures that the ice crystals are as tiny as possible.

Sorbet

Making a basic sorbet

SERVES SIX

INGREDIENTS

150–200g | 5–7oz | ¾–1cup CASTER (SUPERFINE) SUGAR

200–300ml | 7–10fl oz | ¾–1¼ cups WATER

FLAVOURING

1 EGG WHITE

FRUIT PURÉES

As an approximate guide, 500g | 1¼ lb | 5 cups of berry fruits will produce about 450ml | ¾ pint | scant 2 cups purée. Mix this with 115g–150g | 4–5oz | generous ½–¾ cup caster sugar (depending on the natural acidity of the fruit), which has been dissolved in 300ml | ½ pint | 1¼ cups boiling water and then made up to 1 litre | 1¾ pints | 4 cups with extra cold water, lemon or lime juice.

1 Put the sugar and water in a medium pan and heat the mixture, stirring, until the sugar has just dissolved.

2 Add pared citrus rinds, herbs or spices, depending on your chosen flavouring. Leave for 30 minutes to infuse. Strain and cool, then chill well . Mix with additional flavourings such as fruit juices, sieved puréed fruits, herbs or tea.

3 USING AN ICE CREAM MAKER: Pour the syrup mixture into the machine and churn until it is thick but still too soft to scoop.

4 USING AN ICE CREAM MAKER: Lightly beat the egg white with a fork and pour it into the ice cream maker, either adding it through the top vent or removing the lid and stirring it in, depending on the method recommended by the manufacturer of your machine. Continue churning the sorbet until it is firm enough to scoop with a spoon.

5 BY HAND: Pour the mixture into a plastic tub or similar freezerproof, preferably stainless steel, container. It should not be more than 4cm | 1½in deep. Cover and freeze in the coldest part of the freezer for 4 hours or until it has partially frozen and ice crystals have begun to form. Beat until smooth with a fork or hand-held electric whisk. Alternatively, process in a food processor until smooth.

6 BY HAND: Lightly beat the egg white and stir it into the sorbet. Freeze for a further 4 hours or until firm enough to scoop.

COOK'S TIP *If making by hand, ensure that the freezer temperature is as low as possible to speed up the freezing process, and beat at regular intervals, approximately every hour.*

Granitas

Making a citrus granita

This wonderfully refreshing, simple Italian-style water ice has the fine texture of snow and is most often served piled into pretty glass dishes. You don't need fancy or expensive equipment, just a medium pan, a sieve or blender for puréeing the fruit, a fork and room in the freezer for a large plastic container.

INGREDIENTS

There are no hard-and-fast rules when it comes to the proportions of sugar to water, nor is there a standard amount of flavouring that must be added. Unlike sorbets or sherbets, granitas consist largely of water, with just enough sugar to sweeten them and prevent them from freezing too hard. A total of 1 litre | 1¾ pints | 4 cups of flavoured sugar syrup will provide six generous portions of granita.

1 Grate the rind and squeeze the juice from six lemons, six oranges or four ruby grapefruit. Add 115–200g | 4–7oz | generous ½–1 cup caster (superfine) sugar, depending on the acidity of the fruit. Dissolve the sugar in 300ml | ½ pint | 1¼ cups boiling water, then mix it with the citrus juice and rind. Top up to 1 litre | 1¾ pints | 4 cups with extra water or water and alcohol. Add enough alcohol to taste but don't be overgenerous or the granita will not freeze.

2 Pour the chilled mixture into a large plastic tub or similar freezerproof container. It should not be more than 2–2.5cm | ¾–1in deep. Freeze in the coldest part of the freezer for 2 hours until it is mushy around the edges.

Take the container out of the freezer and beat the granita well with a fork to break up the ice crystals. Return the granita to the freezer. Beat it at 30-minute intervals for the next 2 hours until it has the texture of snow.

Making a hot infusion

Some of the most delicious granitas are based on hot mixtures. Coffee is just one example. Pour hot, strong filtered coffee into a bowl or pan and stir in sugar to taste. For a ginger granita, infuse finely chopped fresh root ginger in boiling water, then sweeten it. Chocolate granita is made by mixing cocoa (unsweetened) powder to a smooth paste with a little boiling water and sweetening to taste. All hot infusions must be left to cool, then chilled in the refrigerator before being frozen.

Making a fruit-flavoured granita

To make a fruit-flavoured granita, purée berry fruits such as raspberries or strawberries, then strain the purée to remove the seeds. Alternatively, purée ripe peaches, then strain to remove the skins. To make a melon granita, scoop the seeds out of orange- or green-fleshed melons, then purée the flesh. Peeled and seeded watermelon can be puréed in the same way, or the flesh can be puréed along with the seeds and then strained afterwards.

SERVING AND STORING GRANITAS

Coffee granita is classically served in a tumbler with a spoonful of whipped cream on top. Other types of granita look pretty spooned into tall glasses and decorated with fresh fruits or herb leaves and flowers. Because of its soft, snow-like texture, a granita is best served as soon as it is made. If this is not possible, you can leave it for a couple of hours in the freezer, beating it once or twice more if convenient. If you must freeze a granita overnight or for even longer, let it thaw slightly and beat it really well with a fork before serving. The ice crystals will become smaller but the taste will be the same. As a granita does not contain dairy products there are fewer concerns with food contamination or deterioration.

COOK'S TIP *Before you make the granita, make sure that the container you choose will fit in your freezer. A new stainless steel roasting tin can be used to freeze the granita mixture. As this metal is such a good conductor the granita will freeze very much faster than it would in a plastic container. Do not use aluminium as the metal could react with the fruit acids to give a metallic taste to the finished granita.*

Baskets and biscuits

Not only beautiful to look at, these sensational edible containers are easy to make and bound to impress your guests. They are the ultimate in stylish and professional presentation.

How to make baskets

Spun sugar baskets

These impressive baskets look stunning filled with ice cream or upturned and placed over a single scoop of ice cream to form a cage and arranged in the centre of a large white dinner plate. Use an oiled soup ladle instead of oranges for slightly flatter baskets, and loosen with the tip of a small knife before removing. Add rich colour by decorating the plate with tiny clusters of blueberries, a few raspberries and a sprig or two of redcurrants or any combination of summer fruits. Dust lightly with sugar for the final effect.

MAKES SIX

INGREDIENTS

3 ORANGES, to use as moulds

a little OIL, for greasing

250g | 9oz | generous 1 cup GRANULATED SUGAR

75ml | 5 tbsp WATER

VANILLA ICE CREAM and
FRESH SUMMER FRUITS, to serve

ICING (CONFECTIONERS') SUGAR, for dusting

1 Smooth squares of foil over three oranges and brush lightly with oil. Put the granulated sugar and water in a pan and heat gently, without stirring, until the sugar has completely dissolved. Increase the heat and boil the syrup until it turns golden and starts to caramelize.

2 Take the pan off the heat and plunge the base of the pan into a bowl of cold water to prevent the caramel from overbrowning. Allow the caramel to cool for 15–30 seconds, stirring it gently until it starts to thicken, then lift the pan out of the water.

3 Hold a foil-wrapped orange over the pan and quickly drizzle caramel from a dessertspoon over half the orange, making squiggly lines and gradually building up layers to make the basket shape. Leave the caramel to set and make a second and third basket in the same way. Warm the caramel when it gets too stiff to drizzle.

4 Ease the foil off the first orange. Carefully peel the foil away and put the finished sugar basket on a lightly oiled baking sheet. Repeat with the remaining baskets, then make three more in the same way, reheating the caramel as needed and adding a little boiling water if it becomes too thick to drizzle.

5 Use the baskets on the day you make them, filling them with vanilla ice cream and summer fruits and adding a dusting of sifted icing sugar. The baskets are extremely fragile, so scoop the ice cream on to a plate or baking sheet first and lower it carefully into each basket with the aid of two forks.

Chocolate tulips

These easy-to-make tulip baskets take only minutes to prepare and can then be set aside to harden. Fill with one large scoop of ice cream and decorate with blueberries and halved strawberries, or fill with tiny scoops of ice cream shaped with a melon baller and decorate with tiny chocolate shapes.

VARIATIONS *Any of the chocolate basket ideas suggested here are a perfect way of setting off your favourite chocolate, coffee or vanilla ice cream. You do not have to use dark chocolate to make the baskets – Belgian white or milk chocolate work just as well.*

1 Using the back of a teaspoon, spread 175g | 6oz melted dark (bittersweet) chocolate over six 13cm | 5in circles of non-stick baking parchment, taking it almost, but not completely, to the edge, and giving it a swirly, wave-like edge.

2 Drape each paper circle, chocolate side outwards, over an upturned glass tumbler set on a baking sheet. Ease the paper into soft pleats and leave the baskets in a cool place to set. When ready to serve, lift the baskets off the glasses and carefully peel away the paper.

A large chocolate bowl

3 Chill well until set, then carefully peel away the foil and place the bowl on a plate. Store in the refrigerator until ready to fill with ice cream.

COOK'S TIP *This bowl can be made in any size. Small ones are perfect for individual portions, while larger bowls can serve up to four. Make it thicker than the other bowls and don't fill it too full or the weight of the ice cream might cause the chocolate to crack.*

1 Smooth a double thickness of foil into a suitably sized mixing bowl or basin, so that it takes on the shape of the container. Carefully lift the foil out of the bowl.

2 Spoon melted chocolate into the base of the foil bowl. Spread it to an even, fairly thick layer, taking it over the base and sides with the back of a spoon or a pastry brush.

Individual chocolate cups

3 Fill each of the set chocolate cups with a little parfait. Chill again in the freezer, then carefully peel away the paper from each cup. Use a palette knife to transfer each filled cup to a plate, decorate with a light dusting of sifted cocoa powder (unsweetened) and serve.

COOK'S TIP *When melting chocolate, it is important that the chocolate isn't overheated or allowed to come into contact with steam or small amounts of moisture, as these will cause it to stiffen or "seize". Make sure that the base of the bowl doesn't touch the water and don't allow the water to boil.*

1 Cut six 30 x 15cm | 12 x 6in strips of non-stick baking parchment. Fold each strip in half lengthways, roll into a circle and fit it inside a 7.5cm | 3in plain biscuit (cookie) cutter to make a collar. Secure with tape. Ease the cutter away and make five more collars, leaving the last collar inside the cutter. Place on a baking sheet.

2 Melt 250g/9oz dark chocolate in a heatproof bowl over a pan of hot water. Brush chocolate evenly over the base and sides of the paper collar, supported by the biscuit cutter, and make the top edge jagged. Carefully lift off the biscuit cutter and slide over the next paper collar. Make six cups and leave to set.

How to make biscuits

Tuile biscuits

These classic French biscuits (cookies) are named after the similarly shaped roof tiles found on many old French homes. They are shaped by being draped over a rolling pin as they cool.

SERVES SIX

INGREDIENTS

a little OIL, for greasing

50g | 2oz | ¼ cup UNSALTED (SWEET) BUTTER

75g | 3oz | ¾ cup FLAKED (SLICED) ALMONDS

2 EGG WHITES

75g | 3oz | 6 tbsp CASTER (SUPERFINE) SUGAR

50g | 2oz | ½ cup PLAIN (ALL-PURPOSE) FLOUR, sifted

RIND of ½ ORANGE, finely grated plus 10ml/2 tsp JUICE

SIFTED ICING (CONFECTIONERS') SUGAR, to decorate

1 Preheat the oven to 200°C | 400°F | Gas 6. Lightly brush a wooden rolling pin with oil, and line two large baking sheets with non-stick baking parchment. Melt the butter in a pan then set it aside. Preheat the grill (broiler). Spread out the almonds on a baking sheet and lightly brown under the grill. Leave to cool, then finely grind half; crush the remainder roughly with your fingertips.

2 Put the egg whites and sugar in a bowl and lightly fork them together. Sift in the flour, stir gently to mix, then fold in the melted butter, then the orange rind and juice. Fold in the finely ground nuts.

Cigarettes russes

These biscuits are smaller and rolled more tightly than tuiles, but can be made using the same recipe. Omit the nuts, orange rind and juice and add 5ml | 1 tsp vanilla essence (extract). Make 2–3 biscuits at a time, each time using 10ml | 2 tsp of the mixture spread into a thin circle. The mixture makes 15 cigarettes russes.

3 Drop six teaspoons of the mixture on to one of the lined baking sheets, spacing them well apart. Spread into thin circles and sprinkle lightly with the crushed nuts. Bake in the oven for 5 minutes until just lightly browned around the edges.

COOK'S TIP *It is important to transfer the biscuits to the rolling pin as quickly as possible, because as the biscuits cool they will set and become crisp.*

4 Loosen one of the biscuits with a metal spatula and drape it over the rolling pin. Shape the remaining biscuits in the same way. Leave for 5 minutes to set while baking a second batch. Continue in this way until all the mixture has been used. Dust with icing sugar and serve with ice cream.

Bake the biscuits until they are golden around the edges, then turn them over and wrap them around lightly oiled wooden spoon handles.

Toppings and decorations

Complete the simplest dish of beautifully scooped ice cream or a party-style sundae with one of these professional-looking decorations and you will be sure to impress your dinner guests.

How to make decorations

Plain chocolate caraque

1 Using a metal spatula or the back of a spoon spread melted dark (bittersweet) chocolate over a marble slab or cheese board to a depth of about 5mm | ¼in. Leave in a cool place until set.

2 Draw a long, fine-bladed cook's knife across the chocolate at a 45° angle, using a see-saw action to pare away long curls. If the chocolate is too soft, put it in the refrigerator for just 5 minutes or in a cold place for 15 minutes.

Piped chocolate shapes

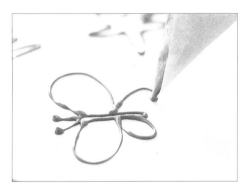

Spoon a little melted dark chocolate into a paper piping (icing) bag and snip off the tip. Pipe squiggly shapes, hearts, butterflies, musical notes or even initials on to a lined baking sheet. Peel off when cool and chill until required.

Two-tone caraque

1 Spoon alternate lines of melted white and dark chocolate over a marble slab or cheese board and spread lightly so that all the chocolate is the same height. Leave to cool and harden.

2 Pare away long, thin curls of chocolate with a fine-bladed cook's knife in the same way as for plain chocolate caraque.

Chocolate rose leaves

Brush melted dark chocolate, as evenly as possible, over the underside of clean, dry rose leaves. Avoid brushing over the edges. Put the leaf on to a non-stick parchment-lined baking sheet and leave in a cool place to set. Carefully peel each leaf away and chill until required.

Simple chocolate curls

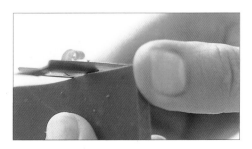

Holding a bar of dark, white or milk chocolate over a plate, pare curls away from the edge of the bar, using a swivel-blade vegetable peeler. Lift the pared curls carefully with a flat blade or a metal spatula and arrange as desired.

COOK'S TIP *If the chocolate used for decoration is not at the right temperature the curls will either be too brittle or won't hold their shape. Set the chocolate aside at room temperature for 20 minutes before using it to make your decorations.*

How to make dipped fruits

Fruit looks and tastes fabulous when half dipped in melted dark (bittersweet) or white chocolate. Choose from tiny strawberries (still with their green hulls attached), tiny clusters of green or red grapes, physalis or cherries, with their stalks. It can also look very effective if you dip half the fruits in dark chocolate and the remainder in white chocolate. Leave the fruits to set on a baking sheet lined with non-stick baking parchment.

Caramel-dipped fruits

For a more unusual fruit decoration for ice cream dishes, half-dip peeled physalis, whole strawberries or cherries (with the stalks intact) into warm syrup, then leave to cool and harden on an oiled baking sheet.

COOK'S TIP *Always carefully select fruit used for decoration, checking that it is perfect and free of any bruising as this will quickly spoil the decoration. Wipe them over with a damp cloth to remove any dust. A more even effect can be achieved if the stalks are still firmly attached to the fruit.*

DECORATING WITH EXOTIC FRUITS

The pretty addition of a few exotic fruits can transform ice cream into a gourmet feast. Physalis look marvellous with their papery cases twisted back to reveal the berry fruit, while pearly white lychees add a dramatic note if the red skin is torn off into a spiral. Try using a quartered fig, with its delicate ruby flesh, or a few jewel-like pomegranate seeds or perfumed passion fruit seeds.

Caramel shapes

The caramel used for making baskets is also suitable for making fancy shapes to decorate ice cream sundaes. Instead of drizzling the caramel on to foil-covered oranges, drizzle shapes such as treble clefs, graduated zigzags, spirals, curly scribbles, initials, stars or hearts on to a lightly oiled baking sheet. Vary the sizes, from small decorations about 5cm|2in long to larger 10cm|4in long shapes.

Using coloured chocolate

1 Pipe random lines of melted dark chocolate over a piece of non-stick baking parchment. Overpipe with white chocolate. Using pink liquid food colouring, tint a little of the melted white chocolate.

2 Pipe a third layer of chocolate squiggles, this time in pink, over the dark and white layers. Chill in the refrigerator until set.

3 Break the coloured shapes into jagged fragments of varying sizes and stick them into ice cream to decorate. They look particularly good on top of ice cream sundaes.

Frosted flowers

1 Lightly beat an egg white, then brush a very thin layer over edible flowers such as pansies, violas, nasturtiums, tiny rose buds or petals. Herb flowers can also be used, as well as strawberries, seedless grapes or cherries.

2 Sprinkle the flower or fruit with caster (superfine) sugar and leave to dry on a large plate. Use on the day of making.

Citrus curls

1 Using a zester, pare the rind of an orange, lemon or lime, removing just the coloured rind of the skin and leaving the bitter white pith on the fruit.

2 Dust the citrus curls with a little caster sugar and use them to sprinkle over citrus-based ices such as lemon sorbet or sherbet.

Corkscrews

1 Use a cannelle knife (zester) to pare long strips of orange, lemon or lime rind. The strips should be as long as possible and very narrow.

2 Twist the strips of rind tightly around cocktail sticks (toothpicks) so that they curl into corkscrews. Hang the corkscrew curls over the edge of ice cream dishes.

Meringue dainties

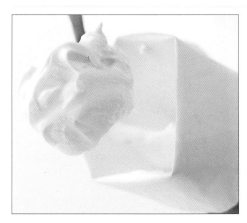

1 Make a meringue mixture using 2 egg whites and 115g|4oz|generous ½ cup caster (super-fine) sugar. Spoon it into a large piping (icing) bag fitted with a small plain 5mm|¼ in nozzle.

2 Pipe heart shapes, zigzags, shooting stars or geometric shapes on to baking sheets lined with non-stick baking parchment.

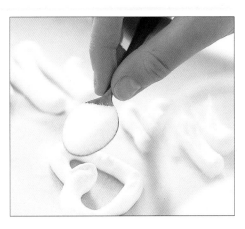

3 Sprinkle the shapes with caster sugar and bake in a low oven until they are firm enough to be lifted off the paper easily. Cool, then store in a container for up to 1 week or until required.

bombes & terrines

Layered, marbled or speckled with fruit and nuts, bombes and terrines make stunning iced desserts that reveal a feast of colour and texture when cut into. Uncomplicated to assemble, but requiring plenty of freezing time, they're best made several days in advance, ready and waiting for that special occasion.

Cassata

Cassata is an irresistible Italian ice cream, usually comprising three layers and frozen in a bombe mould. This version, layered in a terrine, combines the complementary flavours of pistachio, vanilla and tutti frutti.

SERVES EIGHT

INGREDIENTS

6 EGG YOLKS

225g | 8oz | generous 1 cup CASTER (SUPERFINE) SUGAR

15ml | 1 tbsp CORNFLOUR (CORNSTARCH)

600ml | 1 pint | 2½ cups MILK

600ml | 1 pint | 2½ cups DOUBLE (HEAVY) CREAM

75g | 3oz | ¾ cup PISTACHIOS

2.5ml | ½ tsp ALMOND ESSENCE (EXTRACT)

dash each of GREEN and RED FOOD COLOURING

40g | 1½oz | ¼ cup CANDIED PEEL, finely chopped

50g | 2oz | ¼ cup GLACÉ (CANDIED) CHERRIES, washed, dried and finely chopped

5ml | 1 tsp VANILLA ESSENCE (EXRACT)

1 Whisk the egg yolks, sugar, cornflour and a little of the milk until pale and creamy.

2 Bring the remaining milk and the cream to the boil in a large, heavy pan. Immediately whisk into the egg mixture in a steady stream. Return to the pan and cook over a gentle heat, stirring until thickened. Do not let the mixture boil. Divide into three equal quantities, cover and leave to cool.

3 Put the pistachios in a bowl. Cover with boiling water and leave for 1 minute. Drain the nuts and spread between several thicknesses of kitchen paper. Rub between the paper to loosen the skins.

4 Pick out the nuts, rubbing off any remaining skins. Roughly chop and add to one bowl with the almond essence and a drop of green food colouring.

5 Stir the candied peel, glacé cherries and a drop of red food colouring into the second bowl. Stir the vanilla essence into the third. Line a dampened 900g | 2lb terrine or loaf tin (pan) with non-stick baking parchment.

6 BY HAND: Pour the mixtures into 3 separate tubs and freeze them until thickened, beating twice with a fork or in a food processor.

Put the frozen pistachio ice cream into the prepared tin, then the vanilla and the tutti frutti. Freeze overnight until firm.

USING AN ICE CREAM MAKER: Churn the pistachio ice cream in an ice cream maker and spread into the prepared tin. Level the surface. Place in the freezer while preparing the remaining ice creams. Follow the same procedure with the vanilla and then the tutti frutti ice cream. Freeze overnight until firm.

7 To serve, dip the terrine or tin in very hot water for 2–3 seconds, then place a long serving plate upside-down on top of it. Holding together, turn them over. Lift off the container. Peel away the lining paper. Serve the cassata in slices.

Iced Coconut Mousse

Unlike most iced desserts, this is neither cream nor custard based. Instead, creamed coconut is folded

into a very light Italian-style meringue, producing a deliciously aerated, mousse-like texture.

Cream is added, but it does not dominate.

SERVES SIX

INGREDIENTS

4 EGG WHITES

150g | 5oz | ¾ cup CASTER
(SUPERFINE) SUGAR

175g | 6oz | 1½ cups CREAMED
COCONUT (COCONUT CREAM),
grated

300ml | ½ pint | 1¼ cups
DOUBLE (HEAVY) CREAM

15ml | 1 tbsp LEMON JUICE

TOASTED COCONUT SHAVINGS,
to decorate

For the sauce

6 PASSION FRUIT

2.5ml | ½ tsp CORNFLOUR
(CORNSTARCH)

150ml | ¼ pint | ⅔ cup FRESH
ORANGE JUICE

15ml | 1 tbsp CASTER SUGAR

45ml | 3 tbsp KIRSCH

1 Dampen six 150ml | ¼ pint | ⅔ cup metal moulds; line with clear film (plastic wrap). Put the egg whites and sugar in a heatproof bowl over a pan of simmering water. Beat with an electric whisk until thick.

2 Remove from the heat and continue beating for about 2 minutes until the whisk leaves a thick trail when lifted.

3 Fold in the grated coconut. In a separate bowl, whip the cream until it forms soft peaks. Using a large metal spoon, fold the cream and lemon juice into the meringue. Spoon into the prepared moulds.

4 To level, draw a knife across the top of each mould. Cover with clear film and freeze for at least 4 hours or overnight.

5 To make the sauce, cut each passion fruit in half and scoop the seeds and pulp into a small pan. Blend the cornflour with a little of the orange juice in a cup. Stir into the passion fruit mixture, with the remaining orange juice and the sugar. Heat gently, stirring all the time until the mixture thickens slightly. Leave to cool, then stir in the Kirsch.

6 To serve, dip each mould into very hot water for 1 second. Invert the moulds on to dessert plates, lift off the moulds and peel away the clear film. Spoon over a little sauce, decorate with coconut shavings and serve.

COOK'S TIP *Lightly toasting the coconut shavings greatly increases the flavour and works well with the sweetness of the meringue. Spread the coconut shavings on to a lined metal baking sheet and place under a hot grill (broiler) for just a few minutes. Don't leave them for any longer as they will burn very easily and spoil.*

Layered Chocolate and Chestnut Bombes

These delicious little bombes look especially effective if they are served on plates that have been drizzled with melted chocolate, but if you're short of time you can create a very decorative effect simply by dusting the plates with cocoa powder or scattering the bombes with grated chocolate.

SERVES SIX

INGREDIENTS

3 EGG YOLKS

75g | 3oz | 6 tbsp CASTER (SUPERFINE) SUGAR

10ml | 2 tsp CORNFLOUR (CORNSTARCH)

300ml | ½ pint | 1¼ cups MILK

115g | 4oz PLAIN (SEMISWEET) CHOCOLATE, broken into pieces, plus 50g | 2oz, to decorate

150g | 5oz | ½ cup SWEETENED CHESTNUT PURÉE

30ml | 2 tbsp BRANDY or COINTREAU

130g | 4½oz | generous ½ cup MASCARPONE CHEESE

5ml | 1 tsp VANILLA ESSENCE (EXTRACT)

450ml | ¾ pint | scant 2 cups DOUBLE (HEAVY) CREAM

1 Whisk the egg yolks in a bowl with the sugar, cornflour and a little of the milk. Bring the remaining milk to the boil in a heavy pan. Pour the milk over the egg mixture, whisking well. Return to the pan and cook over a very gentle heat, stirring, until thickened. Take care not to boil the custard or it may curdle. Divide the custard equally among three bowls.

2 Add 115g | 4oz of the chocolate to one bowl and leave until melted, stirring frequently until smooth. If the chocolate fails to melt completely, and the bowl is suitable, microwave very briefly.

3 If the chestnut purée is firm, beat it well until softened, then stir it into the second mixing bowl, with the brandy or Cointreau. Add the mascarpone cheese and the vanilla essence to the third bowl of custard. Cover each custard closely with a circle of greaseproof (waxed) paper and leave to cool.

4 Whip the cream until it forms soft peaks. Fold a third of it into each of the cooled custard mixtures. Spoon the chestnut mixture into six 150ml | ¼ pint | ⅔ cup plain or fluted individual moulds and level the surface.

5 Spoon the chocolate mixture over the chestnut mixture in the moulds and level the surface. Spoon the vanilla mixture over the chocolate. Cover and freeze for 6 hours or overnight.

6 To serve, melt the chocolate for decoration in a heatproof bowl set over a pan of gently simmering water. Transfer to a paper piping (icing) bag and snip off the tip. Alternatively use a piping bag fitted with a writing nozzle.

7 Scribble lines of the melted chocolate over the serving plates to decorate. Loosen the edge of each mould with a knife. Dip each mould very briefly in hot water then invert on to a flat surface. Using a metal spatula, carefully transfer the moulds to the serving plates. Leave to stand for 10 minutes at room temperature to allow the ice cream to soften before serving.

VARIATION *If you can't get sweetened chestnut purée use the same quantity of unsweetened purée and add an extra 30ml | 2 tbsp caster sugar.*

Caramel and Pecan Terrine

The combination of caramel and nuts in this dessert is really delicious. Take care that the syrup does not become too dark or the ice cream will taste bitter.

SERVES SIX

INGREDIENTS

115g | 4oz | generous ½ cup
GRANULATED SUGAR

75ml | 5 tbsp WATER

450ml | ¾ pint | scant 2 cups
DOUBLE (HEAVY) CREAM

30ml | 2 tbsp ICING
(CONFECTIONERS') SUGAR

75g | 3oz | ¾ cup PECAN NUTS,
toasted

1 Heat the sugar and water in a small, heavy pan until the sugar dissolves. Boil rapidly until the sugar has turned pale golden. Remove from the heat and leave to stand until the syrup develops a rich brown colour.

2 Pour 90ml | 6 tbsp of the cream over the caramel. Heat to make a smooth sauce. Leave to cool.

3 Dampen a 450g | 1lb loaf tin (pan), then line the base and sides with clear film (plastic wrap). Whip a further 150ml | ¼ pint | ⅔ cup of the cream with the icing sugar until it forms soft peaks. Then whip the remaining cream in a separate bowl and stir in the caramel sauce and pecan nuts.

4 Spoon a third of the caramel cream into the prepared tin and spread with half the plain whipped cream. Spread half of the remaining caramel cream over the top, then top with the last of the plain cream. Finally add the remaining caramel cream and level the surface. Freeze for 6 hours.

5 To serve, dip the tin in very hot water for 2 seconds, invert on to a serving plate and peel away the film. Serve sliced.

COOK'S TIP *Watch the caramel syrup closely after removing it from the heat. If it starts to turn too dark, dip the base of the pan in cold water to arrest the cooking. If the syrup remains very pale, return the pan to the heat and cook the syrup for a little longer.*

Marzipan and Kumquat Terrine

Tangy poached kumquats make a perfect contrast to the sweet almond paste in this

frozen terrine. Any leftover kumquats keep well in the refrigerator for a week,

making a lovely topping for vanilla ice cream.

SERVES SIX

INGREDIENTS

350g | 12oz | 3 cups KUMQUATS

115g | 4oz | generous ½ cup CASTER
(SUPERFINE) SUGAR

150ml | ¼ pint | ⅔ cup WATER

2 EGG YOLKS

10ml | 2 tsp CORNFLOUR
(CORNSTARCH)

300ml | ½ pint | 1¼ cups
FULL-CREAM (WHOLE) MILK

200g | 7oz GOLDEN MARZIPAN

2.5ml | ½ tsp ALMOND ESSENCE

300ml | ½ pint | 1¼ cups
WHIPPING CREAM

1 Cut the kumquats in half and scoop out the seeds with the tip of a knife. Heat the sugar and water gently in a heavy pan until the sugar dissolves. Add the kumquats and cook gently for about 10 minutes until tender. Leave the syrup to cool.

2 . Whisk the egg yolks in a bowl with the cornflour and 60ml | 4 tbsp of the syrup until smooth. In a heavy pan, bring the milk just to the boil, then gradually pour it over the egg yolk mixture, whisking constantly.

3 Return to the pan and cook over a gentle heat for 2 minutes, stirring constantly, until the custard has thickened. Take care not to let the custard boil or it may curdle. Transfer the custard to a bowl. Grate the marzipan and stir in, along with the almond essence (extract). Cover the surface closely with greaseproof (waxed) paper to prevent the formation of a skin on the surface and leave until cold.

4 Line a small terrine or loaf tin with clear film (plastic wrap) and set aside. Put a generous third of the kumquats into a food processor or blender. Pour in a further 60ml | 4 tbsp of the kumquat syrup and blend for a few seconds until smooth and pulpy.

5 BY HAND: Whip the cream until thickened and fold into the custard with the kumquat pulp. Pour into the lined tin and freeze overnight.

USING AN ICE CREAM MAKER: Stir the cream and pulp into the custard and churn until thick. Pour into the tin and freeze for 4 hours.

6 Transfer the tin to the refrigerator about 1 hour before serving to allow it to soften slightly. Invert on to a plate and remove the tin. Peel away the film and serve the ice cream topped with the remaining kumquats.

Spicy Pumpkin and Orange Bombe

Pumpkin has a subtle flavour that is truly transformed with the addition of citrus fruits and spices. Here, the delicious mixture is encased in syrupy sponge and served with an orange and whole spice syrup.

SERVES EIGHT

INGREDIENTS

For the sponge

115g | 4oz | ½ cup UNSALTED (SWEET) BUTTER, softened

115g | 4oz | ½ cup CASTER (SUPERFINE) SUGAR

115g | 4oz | 1 cup SELF-RAISING (SELF-RISING) FLOUR

2.5ml | ½ tsp BAKING POWDER

2 EGGS

For the ice cream

1 ORANGE

300g | 11oz | scant 1½ cups GOLDEN GRANULATED SUGAR

300ml | ½ pint | 1¼ cups WATER

2 CINNAMON STICKS, halved

10ml | 2 tsp WHOLE CLOVES

30ml | 2 tbsp ORANGE FLOWER WATER

400g | 14oz can UNSWEETENED PUMPKIN PURÉE

300ml | ½ pint | 1¼ cups EXTRA THICK DOUBLE (HEAVY) CREAM

2 pieces STEM (CRYSTALLIZED) GINGER, grated

ICING (CONFECTIONERS') SUGAR, for dusting

1 Preheat the oven to 180°C | 350°F | Gas 4. Grease and line a 450g | 1lb loaf tin (pan). Beat the softened butter, caster sugar, flour, baking powder and eggs in a bowl until creamy.

2 Scrape the mixture into the prepared tin, level the surface and bake for 30–35 minutes until firm in the centre. Leave to cool.

3 Make the ice cream. Pare thin strips of rind from the orange, scrape off any white pith, then cut the strips into very fine shreds. Squeeze the orange and set the juice aside. Heat the sugar and water in a small, heavy pan until the sugar dissolves. Bring to the boil and boil rapidly without stirring for 3 minutes.

4 Stir in the orange shreds, juice, cinnamon and cloves and heat gently for 5 minutes. Strain the syrup, reserving the orange shreds and spices. Measure 300ml | ½ pint | 1¼ cups of the syrup and reserve. Return the spices to the remaining syrup and stir in the orange flower water. Pour into a jug and set aside to cool.

5 Beat the pumpkin purée with 175ml | 6fl oz | ¾ cup of the measured strained syrup until evenly combined. Stir in the cream and ginger. Cut the cake into 1cm | ½in slices. Dampen a 1.5 litre | 2½ pint | 6¼ cup ovenproof bowl and line it with clear film. Pour the remaining strained syrup into a shallow dish.

6 Dip the cake slices briefly in the syrup and use to line the prepared basin, placing the syrup-coated sides against the bowl. Trim the pieces to fit where necessary, so that the lining is even and any gaps are filled. Chill.

7 BY HAND: Pour the pumpkin mixture into a shallow container and freeze until firm. Scrape the ice cream into the sponge-lined basin, level the surface and freeze until firm, preferably overnight.

USING AN ICE CREAM MAKER: Churn the pumpkin mixture until very thick, then scrape it into the sponge-lined basin. Level the surface and freeze until firm, preferably overnight.

8 To serve, invert the ice cream on to a serving plate. Lift off the bowl and peel away the clear film. Dust with the icing sugar and serve in wedges with the spiced syrup spooned over.

COOK'S TIP *If you prefer a smooth syrup, strain to remove the cinnamon sticks and cloves before spooning it over the bombe.*

Rippled Nectarine and Cream Cheese Terrine

A delicious combination of nectarine ice cream, cream cheese and sugar, swirled together

attractively and set in the corner of a tilted square cake tin to give

an interesting triangular shape.

SERVES SIX TO EIGHT

INGREDIENTS

50g | 2oz | ¼ cup LIGHT
MUSCOVADO (BROWN) SUGAR

7.5ml | 1½ tsp HOT WATER

200g | 7oz | scant 1 cup
CREAM CHEESE

115g | 4oz | 1 cup ICING SUGAR

90ml | 6 tbsp MILK

3 RIPE NECTARINES

10ml | 2 tsp LEMON JUICE

100ml | 3½fl oz | scant ½ cup
EXTRA THICK DOUBLE CREAM

1 Line one half of a 20cm | 8in square cake tin with clear film (plastic wrap). Dissolve the sugar in the water, stirring until it forms a syrup. Beat a quarter of the icing (confectioner's) sugar with the cream cheese until softened and smooth, then beat in the milk.

2 Cut the nectarines in half, cut out the stones, then place in a food processor. Add the lemon juice and remaining icing sugar and process to a smooth purée.

3 Whip the double (heavy) cream, then fold in the nectarine purée. Prop up the tin at 45°. Spoon in a third of the nectarine purée. Place spoonfuls of the cheese mixture on top.

4 Drizzle with half the sugar syrup. Spoon half the remaining nectarine mixture into the tin, then spoon over the remaining cream cheese and syrup. Finally spoon over the remaining nectarine mixture.

5 Using a dessertspoon handle, fold the mixtures together in about six strokes to lightly ripple the ingredients. Freeze overnight, keeping the tin propped at the same angle in the freezer until solid, then lay the tin flat.

6 Transfer the terrine to the refrigerator about 30 minutes before serving so that it softens. Turn out on to a serving plate and peel away the clear film. Serve in slices.

COOK'S TIP *Before making this dessert, check that the tin (pan) will fit at an angle in the freezer. If not, use a 900g | 2lb loaf tin instead.*

Mocha, Prune and Armagnac Terrines

A really simple iced dessert that is perfect for entertaining. Just remember to allow time for the prunes to soak in the Armagnac.

SERVES SIX

INGREDIENTS

115g | 4oz | ½ cup READY-TO-EAT PITTED PRUNES, chopped

90ml | 6 tbsp ARMAGNAC

90g | 3½oz | ½ cup CASTER (SUPERFINE) SUGAR

150ml | ¼ pint | ⅔ cup WATER

45ml | 3 tbsp COFFEE BEANS

150g | 5oz PLAIN (SEMISWEET) CHOCOLATE, broken into pieces

300ml | ½ pint | 1¼ cups DOUBLE (HEAVY) CREAM

COCOA POWDER, for dusting

1 Put the prunes in a small bowl. Pour over 75ml | 5 tbsp of the Armagnac and leave to soak for at least 3 hours, or overnight in the refrigerator. Line the bases of six 100ml | 3½fl oz | scant ½ cup ramekins with circles cut from greaseproof (waxed) paper.

2 Put the sugar and the measured water in a heavy pan and heat gently until the sugar dissolves, stirring occasionally. Add the soaked prunes and any of the Armagnac that remains in the bowl; simmer the prunes gently in the syrup for 5 minutes.

3 Using a slotted spoon, lift the prunes out of the pan and set them aside. Add the coffee beans to the syrup and simmer gently for 5 minutes.

4 Lift out the coffee beans and put about a third of them in a bowl. Spoon over 120ml | 4fl oz | ½ cup of the syrup and stir in the remaining Armagnac.

5 Add the chocolate to the pan containing the remaining syrup and leave until melted. Whip the cream until it just holds its shape. Using a large metal spoon, fold the chocolate mixture and prunes into the cream until just combined. Spoon the mixture into the lined ramekins, cover and freeze for at least 3 hours.

6 To serve, loosen the edges of the ramekins with a knife then dip in very hot water and invert on to serving plates. Decorate the plates with coffee bean syrup and cocoa powder (unsweetened).

COOK'S TIP *Both the individual terrines and the coffee bean syrup can be made several days in advance if you want to save last-minute cooking. Cover the syrup and store in the refrigerator.*

VARIATION *Armagnac has a smoother, fruitier flavour than ordinary brandy, although brandy makes a good substitute. Real coffee lovers might even like to substitute Kahlúa or another coffee-based liqueur.*

Coconut and Lemon Grass Ice Cream

Lemon grass adds an exotic fragrance to ice creams and sorbets. If you can't get fresh, use the dried stalks or preserved stalks in jars.

SERVES FIVE TO SIX

INGREDIENTS

4 LEMON GRASS STALKS

400ml | 14fl oz | 1⅔ cups
COCONUT MILK

3 EGG YOLKS

90g | 3½oz | ½ cup CASTER
(SUPERFINE) SUGAR

10ml | 2 tsp CORNFLOUR
(CORNSTARCH)

150ml | ¼ pint | ⅔ cup
WHIPPING CREAM

finely grated rind of 1 LIME

For the lime syrup

75g | 3oz | 6 tbsp CASTER SUGAR

75ml | 5 tbsp WATER

1 LIME, very thinly sliced,
plus 30ml | 2 tbsp LIME JUICE

1 Cut the lemon grass stalks in half lengthways and bruise the stalks with a rolling pin. Put them in a heavy pan, add the coconut milk and bring to just below boiling point. Remove from the heat and leave to infuse for 30 minutes, remove the lemon grass.

2 Whisk the egg yolks in a bowl with the sugar and cornflour until smooth. Gradually add the coconut milk, whisking constantly.

3 Return to the pan and heat gently, stirring until the custard thickens. Strain into a clean bowl. Cover with greaseproof (waxed) paper and chill.

4 BY HAND: Lightly whip the cream, add the grated lime rind and fold into the custard. Pour into a container and freeze for 3–4 hours, beating twice as it thickens. Spoon into dariole moulds and return to the freezer for 3 hours.

USING AN ICE CREAM MAKER: Stir the cream and lime rind into the custard. Churn until thick, then spoon into 5–6 dariole moulds. Freeze for at least 3 hours.

5 Heat the sugar and water in a heavy pan until the sugar dissolves. Boil for 5 minutes without stirring. Reduce the heat, add the lime slices and juice and simmer for 5 minutes more. Cool.

6 To turn out, loosen with a knife and briefly dip in very hot water. Serve with syrup and lime slices.

Walnut Castles

This recipe is loosely based on a classic Indian kulfi, using finely chopped walnuts instead of the more familiar pistachio nuts.

SERVES SIX

INGREDIENTS

2 litres | 3½ pints | 9 cups
FULL-CREAM (WHOLE) MILK

15 whole CARDAMOM PODS

75g | 3oz | 6 tbsp CASTER
(SUPERFINE) SUGAR

115g | 4oz | 1 cup WALNUTS,
finely chopped

30ml | 2 tbsp ROSE WATER

15ml | 1 tbsp LEMON JUICE

CHOPPED WALNUTS,
to decorate

1 Put the milk and cardamom pods in a large, heavy pan. Bring to the boil, then simmer vigorously without boiling over. Continue until reduced to about 750ml | 1¼ pints | 3 cups.

2 Strain the milk into a bowl, discarding the cardamom pods. Add the caster sugar, walnuts and rose water and leave to cool then stir in the lemon juice.

BY HAND: Pour the mixture into a shallow container and freeze until thickened and firm.

USING AN ICE CREAM MAKER: Churn the mixture until thick. Spoon into six 120ml | 4fl oz | ½ cup dariole moulds or plastic cups and freeze overnight.

3 To serve, briefly dip the moulds in very hot water, then turn out on to individual dessert plates. Serve scattered with chopped walnuts.

tortes & gâteaux

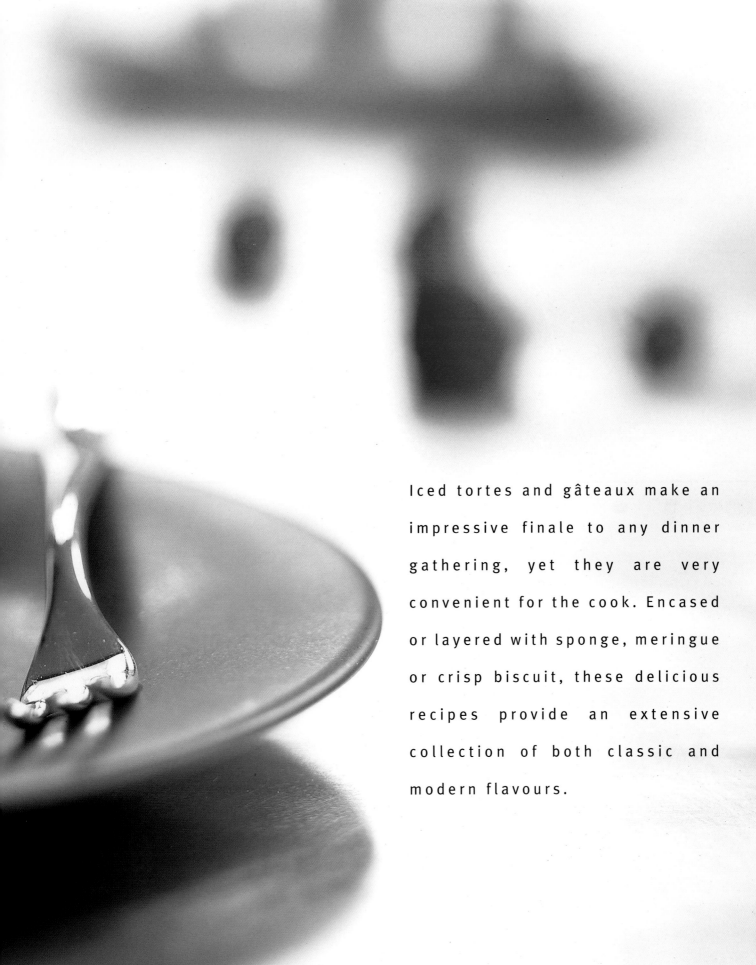

Iced tortes and gâteaux make an impressive finale to any dinner gathering, yet they are very convenient for the cook. Encased or layered with sponge, meringue or crisp biscuit, these delicious recipes provide an extensive collection of both classic and modern flavours.

Zabaglione Ice Cream Torte

For anyone who likes zabaglione, the famous, whisked Italian dessert, this simple iced version is an absolute
must! Its taste and texture are just as good, and there's no last-minute whisking to worry about.

SERVES TEN

INGREDIENTS

175g | 6oz AMARETTI

115g | 4oz | ½ cup READY-TO-EAT
DRIED APRICOTS, finely chopped

65g | 2½oz | 5 tbsp UNSALTED
(SWEET) BUTTER, melted

For the ice cream

65g | 2½oz | 5 tbsp LIGHT
MUSCOVADO (BROWN) SUGAR

75ml | 5 tbsp WATER

5 EGG YOLKS

250ml | 8fl oz | 1 cup
DOUBLE (HEAVY) CREAM

75ml | 5 tbsp MADEIRA OR CREAM
SHERRY

For the apricot compote

150g | 5oz | generous ½ cup READY-
TO-EAT DRIED APRICOTS

25g | 1oz | 2 tbsp LIGHT
MUSCOVADO SUGAR

150ml | ¼ pint | ⅔ cup WATER

1 Put the amaretti in a strong
plastic bag and crush finely with a
rolling pin. Tip into a bowl and
stir in the apricots and melted
butter until evenly combined.

2 Using a dampened dessertspoon,
pack the mixture evenly into the
base and up the sides of a
24cm | 9½in loose-based flan tin
(pan) about 4cm | 1½in deep. Chill.

3 Make the ice cream. Put the
sugar and water in a small, heavy
pan and heat, stirring, until the
sugar has dissolved. Bring to the
boil and boil for 2 minutes without
stirring. Meanwhile bring a large
pan of water to simmering point.
Put the yolks in a heatproof bowl
to fit over the pan without
touching the water.

4 Off the heat, whisk the egg
yolks until pale, then gradually
whisk in the sugar syrup. Put the
bowl over the pan of simmering
water and continue to whisk for
about 10 minutes or until the
mixture leaves a trail when the
whisk is lifted.

5 Remove the bowl from the heat
and carry on whisking for a further
5 minutes or until the mixture is
cold. In a separate bowl, whip the
cream with the Madeira or sherry
until it stands in peaks.

6 Using a large metal spoon, fold
the cream into the whisked
mixture. Spoon it into the amaretti
case, level the surface, cover and
freeze overnight.

7 To make the compote, simmer
the apricots and sugar in the water
until the apricots are plump and
the juices are syrupy, adding a
little more water if necessary.
Leave to cool.

8 Serve the torte in slices with a
little of the compote spooned over
each portion.

Chocolate and Brandied Fig Torte

*A seriously rich torte for chocolate lovers. If you are
not keen on figs, use prunes, dried dates
or apricots instead.*

SERVES EIGHT

INGREDIENTS

250g | 9oz | 1½ cups DRIED FIGS

60ml | 4 tbsp BRANDY

200g | 7oz GINGER NUT BISCUITS

175g | 6oz | ¾ cup UNSALTED
(SWEET) BUTTER, softened

150ml | ¼ pint | ⅔ cup MILK

250g | 9oz PLAIN (SEMISWEET)
CHOCOLATE, broken into pieces

45ml | 3 tbsp CASTER
(SUPERFINE) SUGAR

COCOA POWDER
(UNSWEETENED), for dusting

1 Chop the figs and put them into
a bowl, pour over the brandy and
leave for 2–3 hours until most of
the brandy has been absorbed.
Break the ginger nut biscuits
(gingersnaps) into large chunks,
put them in a strong plastic bag
and crush them with a rolling pin.

2 Melt half the butter and stir in
the biscuit crumbs until combined.
Pack firmly into the base and up
the sides of a 20cm | 8in loose-
based flan tin (pie pan), which is
about 3cm | 1¼in deep. Chill.

3 Pour the milk into a pan, add the
chocolate pieces and heat gently
until the chocolate has melted and
the mixture is smooth, stirring
frequently. Pour the chocolate
mixture into a mixing bowl and
leave to cool.

4 In a separate bowl, beat the
remaining butter with the caster
sugar until the mixture is pale
and creamy.

5 Add the chocolate mixture,
whisking until it is well mixed.
Fold in the figs, and any remaining
brandy, and spoon the mixture into
the biscuit case. Level the surface,
cover and freeze overnight.

6 Transfer to the refrigerator
about 30 minutes before serving so
that the filling softens slightly.
Dust lightly with cocoa powder
and serve in slices, with lightly
whipped cream or crème fraîche.

Rhubarb and Ginger Wine Torte

Rhubarb is not often used in iced desserts, but this luxurious torte uses it in a classic partnership with ginger.

The result is a refreshingly tart flavour, making it the perfect

choice for those who prefer less sweet desserts.

SERVES EIGHT

INGREDIENTS

500g | 1¼lb RHUBARB, trimmed

115g | 4oz | ½ cup CASTER
(SUPERFINE) SUGAR

30ml | 2 tbsp WATER

200g | 7oz | scant 1 cup
CREAM CHEESE

150ml | ¼ pint | ⅔ cups
DOUBLE (HEAVY) CREAM

40g | 1½oz | ¼ cup STEM
(CRYSTALLIZED) GINGER,
finely chopped

a few drops of PINK FOOD
COLOURING (optional)

250ml | 8fl oz | 1 cup GINGER WINE

175g | 6oz SPONGE (LADY) FINGERS

FRESH MINT or LEMON BALM
SPRIGS, dusted with icing
(confectioners') sugar, to decorate

1 Chop the rhubarb roughly and put it in a pan with the sugar and water. Cover and cook very gently for 5–8 minutes until just tender. Process in a food processor or blender until smooth. Cool.

2 Beat the cream cheese in a bowl until softened. Stir in the cream, rhubarb purée and ginger, then a little food colouring, if you like. Line a 900g/2lb/6-8 cup loaf tin (pan) with clear film (plastic wrap).

3 BY HAND: Pour the mixture into a shallow container and freeze until firm.

USING AN ICE CREAM MAKER:
Churn the mixture in an ice cream maker until firm.

4 Pour the ginger wine into a shallow dish. Spoon a thin layer of ice cream over the base of the tin. Working quickly, dip the sponge fingers in the ginger wine, then lay them lengthways over the ice cream in a single layer (*left*). Trim the sponge fingers to fit.

5 Spread another layer of ice cream over the sponge fingers. Repeat, adding two to three more layers and finishing with ice cream. Cover and freeze overnight.

6 Transfer to the refrigerator 30 minutes before serving, to soften the torte slightly. Dip in hot water then invert on to a flat dish. Peel off the clear film and decorate.

COOK'S TIP *Taste the rhubarb mixture just before churning it and add a little icing sugar if you find the flavour overly tart.*

Iced Christmas Torte

Not everyone likes traditional Christmas pudding. This makes an exciting alternative but don't feel that you have to limit it to the festive season. Packed with dried fruit and nuts, it is perfect for any special occasion and looks and tastes sensational.

SERVES EIGHT TO TEN

INGREDIENTS

75g | 3oz | ¾ cup DRIED CRANBERRIES

75g | 3oz | scant ½ cup PITTED PRUNES

50g | 2oz | ⅓ cup SULTANAS (GOLDEN RAISINS)

175ml | 6fl oz/ | ¾ cup PORT

2 pieces STEM (CRYSTALLIZED) GINGER, finely chopped

25g | 1oz | 2 tbsp UNSALTED (SWEET) BUTTER

45ml | 3 tbsp LIGHT MUSCOVADO (BROWN) SUGAR

90g | 3½oz | scant 2 cups FRESH WHITE BREADCRUMBS

600ml | 1 pint | 2½ cups DOUBLE (HEAVY) CREAM

30ml | 2 tbsp ICING (CONFECTIONERS') SUGAR

5ml | 1 tsp MIXED (APPLE PIE) SPICE

75g | 3oz | ¾ cup BRAZIL NUTS, finely chopped

SUGARED BAY LEAVES (see Cook's Tip) and FRESH CHERRIES, to decorate

1 Process the cranberries, prunes and sultanas in a food processor briefly. Put in a bowl; add the port and ginger. Leave to absorb the port for 2 hours.

2 Melt the butter in a frying pan. Add the sugar and heat gently to dissolve. Add the breadcrumbs and fry gently for 5 minutes to colour and crisp. Cool.

3 Process the breadcrumbs in a food processor or a blender and process to fine crumbs. Sprinkle a third into an 18cm/7in loose-based springform tin (pan) and freeze.

4 Whip the cream with the icing sugar and mixed spice until the mixture is thick but not yet standing in peaks. Fold in the brazil nuts with the dried fruit mixture and any port that has not been absorbed.

5 Spread a third of the mixture over the breadcrumb base in the tin, taking care not to dislodge the crumbs. Sprinkle with another layer of the breadcrumbs. Repeat the layering, finishing with a layer of the cream mixture. Freeze the torte overnight.

6 Make the sugared bay leaves. Chill the torte for about 1 hour before serving, decorated with the sugared bay leaves and some fresh cherries.

COOK'S TIP *To make the sugared bay leaves wash and dry the leaves, then paint both sides with beaten egg white. Sprinkle with caster sugar. Dry on greaseproof (waxed) paper for 3 hours.*

Pistachio Nut and Nougat Torte

Pistachio nuts, nougat, honey and rose water make a perfect blend of flavours in this quick and easy torte. Transfer to the refrigerator an hour before serving.

SERVES EIGHT

INGREDIENTS

75g | 3oz | ¼ cup
PISTACHIO NUTS

150g | 5oz NOUGAT

300ml | ½ pint | 1¼ cups
WHIPPING CREAM

90ml | 6 tbsp CLEAR HONEY

30ml | 2 tbsp ROSE WATER

250g | 9oz | generous 1 cup
FROMAGE FRAIS
(RICOTTA CHEESE)

8 TRIFLE SPONGES

ICING (CONFECTIONERS')
SUGAR, for dusting

FRESH RASPBERRIES,
POACHED APRICOTS or
CHERRIES, to serve (optional)

1 Soak the pistachios in boiling water for 2 minutes. Drain them thoroughly, then rub them between pieces of kitchen paper to remove the skins. Peel off any skins that remain, then chop them roughly.

2 Using a small sharp knife or scissors cut the nougat into small pieces. Pour the cream into a bowl, add the honey and rose water and whip until just beginning to hold its shape.

3 Stir in the fromage frais, chopped pistachios and nougat, and mix well. Slice the trifle sponges horizontally into three very thin layers.

4 Line a 15–17cm | 6–6½in square loose-based cake tin (pan) with clear film (plastic wrap). Arrange a layer of sponges on the base, trimming the pieces to fit neatly.

5 Pack the prepared filling into the tin and level the surface. Cover with the remaining sponges, then cover and freeze overnight.

6 To serve, invert the torte on to a serving plate and dust with icing sugar. Serve with raspberries, poached apricots or cherries, if you like.

White Chocolate and Brownie Torte

This is a deliciously easy dessert, guaranteed to appeal to just about everyone! If you can't buy good-quality brownies, use a moist chocolate sponge.

SERVES TEN

INGREDIENTS

300g/11oz
WHITE CHOCOLATE

600ml/1 pint/2½ cups
DOUBLE (HEAVY) CREAM

250g/9oz
RICH CHOCOLATE BROWNIES

COCOA POWDER
(UNSWEETENED), for dusting

1 Dampen the sides of a 20cm | 8in springform tin (pan) and line with a strip of greaseproof (waxed) paper. Break the chocolate into pieces and place in a small pan. Add 150ml | ¼ pint | ⅔ cup of the cream and heat very gently until the chocolate has melted. Stir until smooth, then pour into a bowl and leave to cool.

2 Break the chocolate brownies into chunky pieces and scatter these on the base of the tin. Pack them down lightly to make a fairly dense base.

3 Whip the remaining cream until it forms peaks, then fold in the white chocolate mixture. Spoon into the tin to cover the layer of brownies, then tap the tin gently on the work surface to level the chocolate mixture. Cover and freeze overnight.

4 Transfer to the refrigerator about 45 minutes before serving. Decorate with a light dusting of cocoa powder before slicing.

Iced Strawberry and Lemon Curd Gâteau

Layer two favourite flavours in this fresh fruit gâteau, which is perfect for summer entertaining and takes only minutes to assemble.

4 Fit the cake in the tin, cut-side down. Freeze the cake for 10 minutes, then spread the strawberry ice cream evenly over the sponge and freeze until firm.

SERVES EIGHT

INGREDIENTS

115g | 4oz | ½ cup UNSALTED (SWEET) BUTTER, softened

115g | 4oz | generous ½ cup CASTER (SUPERFINE) SUGAR

2 EGGS

115g | 4oz | 1 cup SELF-RAISING (SELF-RISING) FLOUR

2.5ml | ½ tsp BAKING POWDER

To finish

500ml | 17fl oz | 2¼ cups STRAWBERRY ICE CREAM

300ml | ½ pint | 1¼ cups DOUBLE (HEAVY) CREAM

200g | 7oz | scant 1 cup GOOD QUALITY LEMON CURD

30ml | 2 tbsp LEMON JUICE

500g | 1¼lb | 5 cups STRAWBERRIES, hulled

25g | 1oz | 2 tbsp CASTER SUGAR

45ml | 3 tbsp COINTREAU or other ORANGE-FLAVOURED LIQUEUR

1 Preheat the oven to 180°C | 350°F | Gas 4. Grease and line a 23cm | 9in round springform cake tin. In a mixing bowl, beat the butter with the sugar, eggs, flour and baking powder until creamy.

2 Spoon the mixture into the prepared tin and bake for about 20 minutes or until just firm. Leave to cool for 5 minutes, then turn the cake out on to a wire rack. Cool completely. Wash and dry the cake tin (pan), ready to use again.

3 Line the sides of the clean cake tin with a strip of non-stick baking parchment. Using a sharp knife, carefully slice off the top of the cake where it has formed a crust. Save this for another purpose.

5 Pour the cream into a bowl, whip it until it forms soft peaks, then fold in the lemon curd and lemon juice. Spoon the mixture over the strawberry ice cream. Cover and freeze overnight.

6 About 45 minutes before you intend to serve the dessert, decorate it and make the sauce. Cut half the strawberries into thin slices. Put the rest in a food processor or blender and add the sugar and liqueur. Purée the mixture to make a sauce.

7 Arrange the sliced strawberries over the frozen gâteau. Serve with the sauce spooned over.

Zucotto

An Italian-style dessert with a rich ricotta, fruit, chocolate and nut filling, zucotto is encased in a moist, chocolate and liqueur-flavoured sponge.

SERVES EIGHT

INGREDIENTS

3 EGGS

75g | 3oz | 6 tbsp CASTER (SUPERFINE) SUGAR

75g | 3oz | ⅔ cup PLAIN (ALL-PURPOSE) FLOUR

25g | 1oz | ¼ cup COCOA POWDER (UNSWEETENED), plus extra for dusting

90ml | 6 tbsp KIRSCH

250g | 9oz | generous 1 cup RICOTTA CHEESE

50g | 2oz | ½ cup ICING (CONFECTIONERS') SUGAR

50g | 2oz PLAIN (SEMISWEET) CHOCOLATE, finely chopped

50g | 2oz | ½ cup BLANCHED ALMONDS, chopped and toasted

75g | 3oz | scant ½ cup NATURAL GLACÉ (CANDIED) CHERRIES, quartered

2 pieces STEM (CRYSTALLIZED) GINGER, finely chopped

150ml | ¼ pint | ⅔ cup DOUBLE (HEAVY) CREAM

1 Preheat the oven to 180°C | 350°F | Gas 4. Grease and line a 23cm | 9in cake tin (pan). Whisk the eggs and sugar in a heatproof bowl over a pan of simmering water until the whisk leaves a trail. Off the heat, whisk for a further 2 minutes.

2 Sift in the flour and cocoa; fold in with a large metal spoon. Spoon into the tin; bake for 20 minutes until just firm. Leave to cool.

3 Cut the cake horizontally into three equal layers. Set aside 30ml | 2 tbsp of the Kirsch then drizzle the remaining Kirsch over the cake layers.

4 Beat the ricotta in a bowl until softened, then beat in the icing sugar, chocolate, almonds, cherries, ginger and reserved Kirsch.

5 Pour the cream into a separate bowl and whip it lightly. Using a large metal spoon, fold the cream into the ricotta mixture. Chill. Cut a 20cm | 8in circle from one sponge layer, using a plate as a guide, and set aside.

6 Use the remaining sponge to make the case for the zucotto. Cut the cake to fit the base of a 2.8–3.4 litre | 5–6 pint | 12½–15 cup freezerproof mixing bowl lined with clear film (plastic wrap). Cut more sponge for the sides, fitting the pieces together and taking them about one-third of the way up.

7 Spoon the ricotta filling into the bowl up to the height of the sponge, and level the surface, using the back of a spoon.

8 Fit the reserved circle of sponge on top of the filling. Trim off the excess sponge around the edges. Cover and freeze overnight.

9 Transfer the zucotto to the refrigerator 45 minutes before serving, so that the filling softens slightly. Invert on to a serving plate and peel away the clear film. Dust with cocoa powder and slice.

Raspberry Mousse Gâteau

A lavish quantity of raspberries gives this gâteau its vibrant colour and full flavour. Make it at the height of summer, when raspberries are plentiful and taste their best.

3 Leave to cool, then remove the cake from the tin and place it on a wire rack. Wash and dry the tin.

4 Line the sides of the tin with a strip of greaseproof (waxed) paper and carefully lower the cake back into it. Freeze until the raspberry filling is ready.

5 Set aside 200g|7oz|generous 1 cup of the raspberries. Put the remainder in a clean bowl, stir in the icing sugar, process to a purée in a food processor or blender. Sieve the purée into a bowl, then stir in the whisky, if using.

SERVES EIGHT TO TEN

INGREDIENTS

2 EGGS

50g|2oz|¼ cup CASTER (SUPERFINE) SUGAR

50g|2oz|½ cup PLAIN (ALL-PURPOSE) FLOUR

30ml|2 tbsp COCOA POWDER (UNSWEETENED)

600g|1lb 5oz|3½ cups RASPBERRIES

115g|4oz|1 cup ICING (CONFECTIONERS') SUGAR

60ml|4 tbsp WHISKY (optional)

300ml|½ pint|1¼ cups WHIPPING CREAM

2 EGG WHITES

1 Preheat the oven to 180°C|350°F|Gas 4. Grease and line a 23cm|9in springform cake tin (pan). Whisk the eggs and sugar in a heatproof bowl set over a pan of gently simmering water until the whisk leaves a trail when lifted. Remove the bowl from the heat and continue to whisk the mixture for 2 minutes.

2 Sift the flour and cocoa powder over the mixture and fold in with a large metal spoon. Spoon the mixture into the tin and spread it gently to the edges. Bake for 12–15 minutes until just firm.

6 Whip the cream to form soft peaks. Whisk the egg whites until stiff. Using a large metal spoon, fold the cream, then the egg whites into the raspberry purée.

7 Spread half the raspberry mixture over the cake. Scatter with the reserved raspberries. Spread the remaining raspberry mixture on top and level the surface. Cover and freeze the gâteau overnight.

8 Transfer the gâteau to the refrigerator an hour before serving. Remove from the tin, place on a serving plate and slice.

Rich Chocolate Mousse Gâteau

Because this gâteau is heavily laced with liqueur, you can easily get away with a bought sponge. The mousse is rich, so serve small portions.

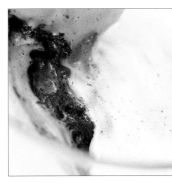

SERVES TWELVE

INGREDIENTS

400g | 14oz CHOCOLATE SPONGE

75ml | 5 tbsp COINTREAU

finely grated rind and juice of
1 ORANGE

300g | 11oz PLAIN (SEMISWEET)
CHOCOLATE, broken into pieces

25g | 1oz | ¼ cup COCOA POWDER
(UNSWEETENED)

45ml | 3 tbsp GOLDEN
(LIGHT CORN) SYRUP

3 EGGS

300ml | ½ pint | 1¼ cups WHIPPING
CREAM

150ml | ¼ pint | ⅔ cup DOUBLE
(HEAVY) CREAM, lightly whipped

COCOA POWDER, for dusting

1 Cut the sponge cake into
5mm | ¼in thick slices. Set a third
aside, and use the remainder to
make a case for the mousse. Line
the base and sides of a 23cm | 9in
loose-based or springform cake tin
(pan) with cake, trimming to fit,
making a sponge case about 4cm |
1½ in deep.

2 Mix 30ml | 2 tbsp of the liqueur
with the orange juice and drizzle
over the sponge case.

3 Put the chocolate in a heatproof
bowl. Add the cocoa powder, syrup
and remaining liqueur and place
the bowl over a pan of gently
simmering water. Leave until the
chocolate has melted, then remove
from the heat. Stir until smooth.

4 Whisk the eggs with the orange
rind in a mixing bowl until they are
thick and pale. Whip the whipping
cream until it forms soft peaks.

5 Fold the chocolate mixture into
the whisked eggs, using a large
metal spoon, then fold in the
whipping cream. Scrape the
mixture into the sponge case and
level the surface.

6 Cover with the reserved
chocolate cake, trimming the pieces
to fit. Cover and freeze overnight.

7 Transfer to the refrigerator
30 minutes before serving. Invert on
to a plate, spread with the double
cream and dust with cocoa powder.

Maple and Walnut Meringue Gâteau

This simple dessert makes a feast for all meringue lovers. Before serving, let it thaw slightly in the refrigerator to enjoy the full flavour.

SERVES TEN TO TWELVE

INGREDIENTS

4 EGG WHITES

200g | 7oz | scant 1 cup
LIGHT MUSCOVADO
(BROWN) SUGAR

150g | 5oz | 1¼ cups
WALNUT PIECES

600ml | 1 pint | 2½ cups
DOUBLE (HEAVY) CREAM

150ml | ¼ pint | ⅔ cup
MAPLE SYRUP,
plus extra, to serve

1 Preheat the oven to 140°C | 275°F | Gas 1. Draw three 23cm | 9in circles on non-stick baking paper. Invert on to three baking sheets. Whisk the egg whites in a bowl until stiff.

2 Whisk in the sugar, about 15ml | 1 tbsp at a time, whisking well after each addition until the meringue is stiff and glossy. Spread to within 1cm | ½in of the edge of each marked circle. Bake for about 1 hour or until crisp, swapping the baking sheets around halfway through cooking. Leave to cool.

3 Set aside 45ml | 3 tbsp of the walnuts. Finely chop the remainder. Whip the cream with the maple syrup until it forms soft peaks. Fold in the chopped walnuts. Use about a third of the mixture to sandwich the meringues together on a flat, freezerproof serving plate.

4 Using a metal spatula, spread the remaining cream mixture over the top and sides of the gâteau. Sprinkle with the reserved walnuts and freeze overnight.

5 Transfer to the refrigerator about 1 hour before serving so that the cream filling softens slightly. Drizzle a little of the extra maple syrup over the top just before serving. Serve in slices.

Soft Fruit and Crushed Meringue Gâteau

This recipe takes five minutes to make but looks and tastes as though a lot of preparation went into it. Use really good quality vanilla ice cream.

SERVES SIX

INGREDIENTS

400g | 14oz | 3½ cups MIXED SMALL
STRAWBERRIES, RASPBERRIES
or REDCURRANTS

30ml | 2 tbsp ICING
(CONFECTIONERS') SUGAR

750ml | 1¼ pints | 3 cups
VANILLA ICE CREAM

6 MERINGUE NESTS

1 Dampen a 900g | 2lb loaf tin (pan) and line with clear film (plastic wrap). Cut the strawberries into small pieces, if using. Put them in a bowl and add the raspberries or redcurrants and icing sugar. Toss until the fruit is beginning to break up but do not let it become mushy.

2 Put the ice cream in a bowl and break it up with a fork. Crumble the meringues into the bowl and add the soft fruit mixture.

3 Fold all the ingredients together until evenly combined and lightly marbled. Pack into the prepared tin and press down gently to level. Cover and freeze overnight. To serve, invert on to a plate and peel away the clear film. Serve in slices.

Brandied Apple Charlotte

Loosely based on a traditional Apple Charlotte, this iced version combines brandy-steeped dried apple with a spicy ricotta cream to make an unusual and very tasty dessert.

SERVES EIGHT TO TEN

INGREDIENTS

130g | 4½oz | ¾ cup
DRIED APPLES

75ml | 5 tbsp BRANDY

50g | 2oz | ¼ cup
UNSALTED (SWEET) BUTTER

115g | 4oz | ½ cup LIGHT
MUSCOVADO (BROWN) SUGAR

2.5ml | ½ tsp
MIXED (APPLE PIE) SPICE

60ml | 4 tbsp WATER

75g | 3oz | ½ cup SULTANAS
(GOLDEN RAISINS)

300g | 11oz MADEIRA CAKE, cut
into 1cm | ½in slices

250g | 9oz | generous 1 cup
RICOTTA CHEESE

30ml | 2 tbsp LEMON JUICE

150ml | ¼ pint | ⅔ cup
DOUBLE (HEAVY) or
WHIPPING CREAM

ICING (CONFECTIONERS')
SUGAR and FRESH MINT SPRIGS,
to decorate

1 Roughly chop the dried apples, then place in a bowl. Pour over the brandy and set aside for about 1 hour until most of the brandy has been absorbed.

2 Melt the butter in a frying pan. Add the sugar and stir over a low heat for 1 minute. Add the mixed spice, water and soaked apples, with any remaining brandy. Cook gently for 5 minutes or until the apples are tender. Stir in the sultanas and leave to cool.

3 Use the cake slices to line the sides of a 20cm | 8in square or 20cm | 8in round springform or loose-based cake tin (pan). Place in the freezer and make the filling.

4 Beat the ricotta in a bowl until it has softened, then stir in the apple mixture and lemon juice. Whip the cream in a separate bowl and fold it in. Spoon the mixture into the lined tin and level the surface. Cover and freeze overnight.

5 Transfer to the refrigerator 1 hour before serving. Invert on to a serving plate, dust with sugar and decorate with mint sprigs.

Chocolate, Rum and Raisin Roulade

SERVES SIX

INGREDIENTS

This richly flavoured dessert can be assembled and frozen a week or two in advance. Use vanilla, chocolate or coffee ice cream if you prefer, though all versions will be just as enjoyably indulgent.

For the roulade

115g | 4oz PLAIN (SEMISWEET) CHOCOLATE, broken into pieces

4 EGGS, separated

115g | 4oz | generous ½ cup CASTER (SUPERFINE) SUGAR

COCOA POWDER (UNSWEETENED) and ICING (CONFECTIONERS') SUGAR, for dusting

For the filling

150ml | ¼ pint | ⅔ cup DOUBLE (HEAVY) CREAM

15ml | 1 tbsp ICING SUGAR

30ml | 2 tbsp RUM

300ml | ½ pint | 1¼ cups RUM AND RAISIN ICE CREAM

1 Make the roulade. Preheat the oven to 180°C | 350°F | Gas 4. Grease a 33 x 23cm | 13 x 9in Swiss roll tin and line with non-stick baking parchment. Grease the parchment. Melt the chocolate in a heatproof bowl set over a pan of simmering water.

2 In a separate bowl, whisk the egg yolks with the caster sugar until thick and pale. Stir the melted chocolate into the yolk mixture. Whisk the egg whites in a grease-free bowl until stiff. Stir a quarter of the whites into the yolk mixture to lighten it, then fold in the remainder.

3 Pour the mixture into the prepared tin and spread it gently into the corners. Bake for about 20 minutes until the cake has risen and is just firm. Turn it out on to a sheet of greaseproof (waxed) paper which has been supported on a baking sheet and generously dusted with caster sugar. Leave to cool, then peel away the lining.

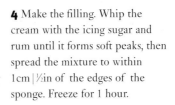

4 Make the filling. Whip the cream with the icing sugar and rum until it forms soft peaks, then spread the mixture to within 1cm | ½in of the edges of the sponge. Freeze for 1 hour.

5 Using a dessertspoon, scoop up long curls of the ice cream and lay an even layer over the cream.

6 Starting from a narrow end carefully roll up the sponge, using the paper to help. Slide the roulade off the paper-lined baking sheet and on to a long plate that is freezerproof. Cover and freeze overnight. Transfer to the refrigerator 30 minutes before serving. Serve dusted with cocoa powder and icing sugar.

hot
ice cream
desserts

There's nothing to beat the soft, melting texture of ice cream as it seeps into a deliciously warm pastry or mingles with the juices of a hot fruit compote, bringing out the flavour of both. The following chapter combines quick-and-easy puddings with make-ahead desserts. Serve immediately to enjoy the lingering warmth.

Baby Alaskas with Liqueured Apricots

Just as effective as a traditional baked Alaska, these individual ices are concealed under their own little meringue mountains.

SERVES SIX

INGREDIENTS

40g | 1½oz | 3 tbsp CASTER (SUPERFINE) SUGAR

60ml | 4 tbsp WATER

150g | 5oz | generous ½ cup READY-TO-EAT DRIED APRICOTS, roughly chopped

30ml | 2 tbsp COINTREAU or other ORANGE-FLAVOURED LIQUEUR

500ml | 17fl oz | 2¼ cups VANILLA, HONEY or any NUT-FLAVOURED ICE CREAM

6 LARGE ALMOND or GINGER BISCUITS (COOKIES)

3 EGG WHITES

175g | 6oz | scant 1 cup CASTER SUGAR

1 Heat the sugar and water in a small, heavy pan, stirring occasionally, until the sugar has dissolved. Add the apricots and simmer gently for 5 minutes until they have absorbed most of the syrup. Stir in the Cointreau liqueur and leave to chill.

2 Freeze six small dariole moulds or metal pudding moulds for 15 minutes. At the same time, remove the ice cream from the freezer and leave for 15 minutes.

VARIATION *Feel free to experiment and substitute your favourite liqueur for the orange one recommended here. You can also use any other dried fruits instead of the apricots, if you prefer.*

3 Using a dessertspoon, pack most of the ice cream into the moulds, leaving a deep cavity in the centre of each. Return each mould to the freezer once completed.

4 When all the moulds have been lined with ice cream, remove them from the freezer again and fill the centres with the apricots. Cover the apricots with more ice cream and freeze until firm.

5 Dip each mould in very hot water for 1–2 seconds, then invert. Slide a biscuit under each ice cream and transfer to a baking sheet. Place in the freezer.

6 Whisk the egg whites in a grease-free bowl until they are stiff. Gradually whisk in the caster sugar, a tablespoonful at a time, whisking well after each addition until the mixture has become stiff and glossy.

7 Using a metal spatula spread a thick layer of the meringue over each ice cream, making sure the meringue meets the biscuits and seals in the ice cream. Swirl the surface decoratively. Return the covered ice creams to the freezer.

8 About 15 minutes before serving, preheat the oven to 230°C | 450°F | Gas 8. Bake the Alaskas for about 2 minutes until the meringue is pale golden. Serve immediately.

Coconut and Passion Fruit Alaska

A really classic ice cream extravaganza, baked Alaska lends itself to many variations on the basic theme.

This version comprises a passion-fruit-steeped coconut sponge, topped with tropical fruit ice

cream and smothered in a delicious coconut-flavoured meringue.

SERVES EIGHT

INGREDIENTS

For the sponge

115g | 4oz | ½ cup UNSALTED (SWEET) BUTTER, softened

115g | 4oz | generous ½ cup CASTER (SUPERFINE) SUGAR

2 EGGS

115g | 4oz | 1 cup SELF-RAISING (SELF-RISING) FLOUR

2.5ml | ½ tsp BAKING POWDER

5ml | 1 tsp ALMOND ESSENCE (EXTRACT)

40g | 1½oz | ½ cup DESICCATED (DRY UNSWEETENED SHREDDED) COCONUT

15ml | 1 tbsp MILK

To finish

1 litre | 1¾ pints | 4 cups PASSION FRUIT, MANGO or TROPICAL FRUIT ICE CREAM

60ml | 4 tbsp KIRSCH

3 PASSION FRUIT

3 EGG WHITES

115g | 4oz | generous ½ cup CASTER SUGAR

50g | 2oz | ½ cup COCONUT CREAM, grated

1 Preheat the oven to 180°C | 350°F | Gas 4. Grease and line an 18cm | 7in round cake tin (pan). Whisk the sponge ingredients together, spoon into the tin, level the surface and bake for 35 minutes until the sponge is just firm. Leave to cool on a wire rack.

2 Dampen a 1.2 litre | 2 pint | 5 cup ovenproof bowl and line it with clear film (plastic wrap). Remove the ice cream from the freezer for 15 minutes to soften slightly.

3 Pack the ice cream into the lined bowl and return to the freezer for 1 hour. Place the sponge on a small baking sheet or ovenproof plate and drizzle the surface with Kirsch. Remove the pulp from the fruit and scoop over the sponge.

4 Dip the bowl containing the ice cream into very hot water for about 2 seconds to loosen the shaped ice cream. Invert on to the sponge. Peel away the clear film and put the cake and ice cream in the freezer.

5 To make the meringue, whisk the egg whites in a clean bowl until stiff. Gradually add the sugar, a tablespoon at a time, whisking well after each addition, until the meringue is thick and glossy. Fold in the grated creamed coconut.

6 Using a metal spatula, spread the meringue over the ice cream and sponge to cover both completely. Return to the freezer.

7 About 15 minutes before serving, preheat the oven to 220°C | 425°F | Gas 7. Bake for 4–5 minutes, watching closely, until the peaks are golden. Serve immediately.

Ice Cream Croissants with Chocolate Sauce

MAKES FOUR

INGREDIENTS

75g | 3oz PLAIN (SEMISWEET) CHOCOLATE, broken into pieces

15g | ½oz | 1 tbsp UNSALTED (SWEET) BUTTER

30ml | 2 tbsp GOLDEN (LIGHT CORN) SYRUP

4 CROISSANTS

90ml | 6 tbsp GOOD QUALITY READY-MADE VANILLA CUSTARD

4 large scoops of VANILLA ICE CREAM

ICING (CONFECTIONERS') SUGAR, for dusting

1 Preheat the oven to 180°C | 350°F | Gas 4. Put the chocolate in a small, heavy pan. Add the butter and syrup and heat very gently until smooth, stirring the mixture frequently.

2 Split the croissants in half horizontally and place the bases on a baking sheet. Spoon the custard over the bases, cover with the lids and bake for 5 minutes until warmed through.

3 Remove the lids and place a scoop of ice cream in each croissant. Spoon half the sauce over the ice cream and press the lids down gently. Bake the croissants for 1 minute more.

4 Dust the filled croissants with icing sugar, spoon over the remaining chocolate sauce and serve immediately.

A deliciously easy croissant "sandwich" with a filling of vanilla custard, ice cream and chocolate sauce melting inside the warmed bread.

Baked Bananas with Ice Cream

Baked bananas make the perfect partners for delicious vanilla ice cream topped with a toasted hazelnut sauce. A quick and easy dessert that looks as good as it tastes.

SERVES FOUR

INGREDIENTS

4 LARGE BANANAS

4 large scoops of VANILLA ICE CREAM

For the sauce

25g | 1oz | 2 tbsp UNSALTED (SWEET) BUTTER

50g | 2oz | ½ cup HAZELNUTS, toasted and roughly chopped

45ml | 3 tbsp GOLDEN (LIGHT CORN) SYRUP

30ml | 2 tbsp LEMON JUICE

1 Preheat the oven to 180°C | 350°F | Gas 4. Place the unpeeled bananas on a baking sheet and brush them with 15ml | 1 tbsp lemon juice. Bake for 20 minutes until the skins are turning black and the flesh gives a little when the bananas are gently squeezed.

COOK'S TIP *Bake the bananas over the dying coals of a barbecue, if you like. Put them on the rack as soon as you have removed all the main course items.*

2 Meanwhile, make the sauce. Melt the butter in a small pan. Add the hazelnuts and cook gently for 1 minute. Add the syrup and lemon juice and heat, stirring, for 1 minute more.

3 To serve, slit each banana open with a knife and open out the skins. Transfer to serving plates and serve with scoops of ice cream. Pour the sauce over.

Filo, Ice Cream and Mincemeat Parcels

MAKES TWELVE

Looking rather like crispy fried pancakes, these golden parcels reveal hot chunky mincemeat and melting vanilla ice cream when cut open. They can be assembled days in advance, ready for easy, last-minute frying.

INGREDIENTS

1 FIRM PEAR

225g | 8oz | 1 cup MINCEMEAT

finely grated rind of 1 LEMON

12 sheets of FILO PASTRY, thawed if frozen

a little beaten EGG

250ml | 8 fl oz | 1 cup VANILLA ICE CREAM

OIL, for deep frying

CASTER (SUPERFINE) SUGAR for dusting

1 Peel, core and chop the pear. Put in a small bowl and then stir in the mincemeat and lemon rind.

2 Lay one filo sheet on the work surface and cut it into two 20cm | 8in squares. Brush one square lightly with beaten egg then cover with the second square.

3 Lay 10ml | 2 tsp mincemeat on the filo, placing it 2.5cm | 1in away from one edge and spreading it slightly to cover a 7.5cm | 3in area. Lay 10ml | 2 tsp of the ice cream over the mincemeat. Brush all around the edges of the filo with beaten egg.

4 Fold over the two opposite sides of the pastry to cover the filling. Roll up the strip, starting from the filled end. Transfer to a baking sheet and freeze. Make 11 more rolls in the same way.

5 When you are ready to serve, pour oil into a heavy pan to a depth of 7.5cm | 3in. Heat to 185°C | 365°F or until a cube of bread added to the oil browns in 30 seconds.

6 Fry several parcels at a time for 1–2 minutes until pale golden, turning them over during cooking. Drain on kitchen paper while frying the remainder. Dust with caster sugar and serve immediately.

COOK'S TIP *Filo pastry sheets vary considerably in size. Don't worry if you can't get two 20cm | 8in squares from each sheet. It won't matter if the squares are slightly smaller or even rectangular as long as they can be rolled to enclose the filling.*

Walnut and Vanilla Ice Palmiers

These walnut pastries can be served freshly baked, but for convenience, make them ahead and reheat them in a moderate oven for 5 minutes.

MAKES SIX

INGREDIENTS

75g | 3oz | ¾ cup WALNUT PIECES

350g | 12oz PUFF PASTRY, thawed if frozen

beaten EGG, to glaze

45ml | 3 tbsp CASTER (SUPERFINE) SUGAR

about 200ml | 7fl oz | scant 1 cup VANILLA ICE CREAM

1 Preheat the oven to 200°C | 400°F | Gas 6. Lightly grease a large baking sheet with butter. Chop the walnuts finely. On a lightly floured surface roll the pastry to a thin rectangle 30 x 20cm | 12 x 8in.

2 Trim the edges of the pastry then brush with the egg. Sprinkle over all but 45ml | 3 tbsp of the chopped walnuts and 30ml | 2 tbsp of the sugar. Run the rolling pin over the walnuts to press them into the pastry.

3 Roll up the pastry from one short side to the centre, then roll up the other side until the two rolls meet. Brush the points where the rolls meet with a little beaten egg. Using a sharp knife, cut the pastry into 1cm | ½in thick slices.

4 Lay the slices on the work surface and flatten them with a rolling pin. Transfer to the baking sheet. Brush with more of the beaten egg and sprinkle with the reserved walnuts and sugar.

5 Bake for about 15 minutes until pale golden. Serve the palmiers warm, in pairs, sandwiched with the vanilla ice cream.

Peach, Blackberry and Ice Cream Gratin

A wonderfully easy dessert in which the flavours of the peaches, blackberries, ice cream and sugar mingle together. Use large, ripe peaches with enough space for the filling.

2 Brush the cut surfaces with lemon juice and transfer to a shallow flameproof dish. Grill (broil) for 2 minutes. Remove from the heat, but leave the grill on to maintain the temperature.

3 Using a small teaspoon, take small scoops of the ice cream and pack them into the peach halves, piling it up in the centre. Add the blackberries, pushing them gently into the ice cream.

4 Sprinkle the filled peaches with the muscovado sugar and replace under the hot grill for 1–2 minutes until the sugar has dissolved and the ice cream is beginning to melt. Serve immediately.

SERVES FOUR

INGREDIENTS

4 LARGE PEACHES

15ml | 1 tbsp LEMON JUICE

120ml | 4fl oz | ½ cup FIRM VANILLA ICE CREAM

115g | 4oz | 1 cup SMALL BLACKBERRIES

40g | 1½oz | 3 tbsp LIGHT MUSCOVADO (BROWN) SUGAR

1 Preheat the grill (broiler). Cut the peaches in half and remove the stones. Cut a thin slice off the rounded side of each peach so that they sit flat on the surface.

COOK'S TIP *Other berries, such as fresh blueberries, can be used instead of blackberries, if you prefer.*

Don't take the ice cream out of the freezer until just before you are ready to fill the peaches, and then work quickly. The ice cream must still be solid or it will melt too quickly when the dessert is under the hot grill.

Apple Ice Cream with Cinnamon Bread

Cooking the apples with butter, lemon and spice accentuates their flavour and makes a marvellous
ice cream. It is good over apple pies and other pastries, but even better
with crisp fried sugared bread.

SERVES SIX

INGREDIENTS

675g | 1½lb COOKING APPLES

50g | 2oz | ¼ cup
UNSALTED (SWEET) BUTTER

1.5ml | ¼ tsp
MIXED (APPLE PIE) SPICE

finely grated rind and juice of
1 LEMON

90g | 3½oz | scant ½ cup
CREAM CHEESE

2 EGG WHITES, beaten

150ml | ¼ pint | ⅔ cup
DOUBLE (HEAVY) CREAM

MINT SPRIGS,
to decorate

For the cinnamon bread

6 thick slices of WHITE BREAD

1 EGG, beaten

1 EGG YOLK

2.5ml | ½ tsp NATURAL
VANILLA ESSENCE (EXTRACT)

150ml | ¼ pint | ⅔ cup
SINGLE (LIGHT) CREAM

65g | 2½oz | 5 tbsp CASTER
(SUPERFINE) SUGAR

2.5ml | ½ tsp GROUND CINNAMON

25g | 1oz | 2 tbsp UNSALTED
BUTTER

45ml | 3 tbsp OIL

1 Peel, core and slice the apples. Melt the butter in a pan. Add the apple, spice and lemon rind. Cover and cook gently for 10 minutes until soft. Cool.

2 Tip the apples and juices into a food processor then the lemon juice and cream cheese. Blend until smooth. In separate bowls, whisk the egg whites until stiff and the cream until it forms soft peaks.

3 Scrape the purée into a bowl. Fold in the cream, then the egg whites. Spoon into a plastic tub and freeze overnight.

4 Make the cinnamon bread about 20 minutes before serving. Cut the crusts off the bread slices, then cut each slice diagonally in half. Beat together the egg, egg yolk, vanilla essence, cream and 15ml | 1 tbsp of the sugar.

5 Arrange the bread triangles in a single layer on a large, shallow plate or tray. Pour the cream mixture over the bread triangles and leave for about 10 minutes until the mixture has been thoroughly absorbed.

6 Mix the remaining sugar with the cinnamon on a plate. Melt the butter in the oil in a large frying pan. When it is hot, add half the bread and fry until golden underneath. Turn with a metal spatula and fry the other side.

7 Drain the slices lightly on kitchen paper, then coat them on both sides in the cinnamon sugar and keep them hot. Cook the remaining slices in the same way. Serve at once, topped with scoops of the apple ice cream. Decorate with the mint sprigs.

Ice Cream with Hot Cherry Sauce

Hot cherry sauce makes a classic yet really simple accompaniment to ice cream for serving on any occasion. Use only good quality chocolate and vanilla.

SERVES FOUR

INGREDIENTS

425g | 15oz can PITTED BLACK CHERRIES

10ml | 2 tsp CORNFLOUR (CORNSTARCH)

finely grated rind of 1 LEMON, plus 10ml | 2 tsp JUICE

15ml | 1 tbsp CASTER (SUPERFINE) SUGAR

2.5ml | ½ tsp GROUND CINNAMON

30ml | 2 tbsp BRANDY or KIRSCH, optional

400ml | 14fl oz | 1⅔ cups DARK (BITTERSWEET) CHOCOLATE ICE CREAM

400ml | 14fl oz | 1⅔ cups VANILLA ICE CREAM

DRINKING CHOCOLATE POWDER, for dusting

1 Drain the cherries, reserving the juice. Spoon the cornflour into a small pan and blend to a paste with a little of the reserved juice from the cherries.

2 Stir in the remaining cherry juice with the lemon rind and juice, sugar and cinnamon. Bring to the boil, stirring, until smooth and glossy.

3 Add the cherries, with the brandy or Kirsch, if using. Stir gently, then cook for 1 minute. Scoop the ice cream into shallow dishes. Spoon the sauce around, dust with chocolate powder and serve.

Syrupy Brioche Slices with Vanilla Ice Cream

Keep a few individual brioche buns in the freezer to make this fabulous five-minute pudding.

SERVES FOUR

INGREDIENTS

BUTTER, for greasing

finely grated rind and juice of 1 ORANGE

50g | 2oz | ¼ cup CASTER (SUPERFINE) SUGAR

90ml | 6 tbsp WATER

1.5ml | ¼ tsp GROUND CINNAMON

4 BRIOCHE BUNS

15ml | 1 tbsp ICING (CONFECTIONERS') SUGAR

400ml | 14fl oz | 1⅔ cups VANILLA ICE CREAM

1 Lightly grease a gratin dish and set aside. Put the orange rind and juice, sugar, water and cinnamon in a heavy pan. Heat gently, stirring, until the sugar has dissolved, then boil for 2 minutes without stirring.

2 Remove the syrup from the heat and pour into a shallow heatproof dish. Preheat the grill (broiler). Cut each brioche vertically into three thick slices. Dip one side of each slice in the hot syrup and arrange in the gratin dish, syrupy sides down. Reserve the remaining syrup. Grill (broil) the brioche until lightly toasted.

3 Turn over and dust with icing sugar. Grill for 2–3 minutes more until they begin to caramelize around the edges.

4 Transfer to serving plates and top with scoops of ice cream. Spoon over the remaining syrup and serve immediately.

Blueberry and Vanilla Crumble Torte

In this heavenly pudding, vanilla ice cream is packed into a buttery crumble case and baked until the ice cream starts to melt over the crumble. Remember that you need to start making this the day before you intend to serve it.

SERVES EIGHT

INGREDIENTS

225g | 8oz | 2 cups PLAIN (ALL-PURPOSE) FLOUR

5ml | 1 tsp BAKING POWDER

175g | 6oz | ¾ cup UNSALTED (SWEET) BUTTER, diced

150g | 5oz | ¾ cup CASTER (SUPERFINE) SUGAR

1 EGG

75g | 3oz | ¾ cup GROUND ALMONDS

10ml | 2 tsp natural VANILLA ESSENCE (EXTRACT)

5ml | 1 tsp MIXED (PUMPKIN PIE) SPICE

500ml | 17fl oz | 2¼ cups VANILLA ICE CREAM

175g | 6oz | 1½ cups BLUEBERRIES

ICING (CONFECTIONERS') SUGAR, for dusting

1 Preheat the oven to 180°C | 350°F | Gas 4. Put the flour and baking powder in a food processor. Add the butter and process briefly to mix. Add the sugar and process briefly again until the mixture is crumbly. Remove about 175g | 6oz | 1½ cups of the crumble mixture and set this aside.

2 Add the egg, ground almonds, vanilla essence and mixed spice to the remaining crumble mixture and blend to a paste.

3 Scrape the paste into a 20cm | 8in springform tin. Press it firmly and evenly into the base and halfway up the sides. Line the pastry case with greaseproof (waxed) paper and fill with baking beans.

4 Sprinkle the crumble mixture on to a baking sheet. Bake the crumble for 20 minutes and the case for about 30 minutes until pale golden. Remove the paper and beans from the case and bake for 5 minutes more. Leave both the crumble and the case to cool.

5 Pack the ice cream into the almond pastry case and level the surface. Scatter with the blueberries and then the baked crumble mixture. Freeze overnight.

6 About 25 minutes before serving, preheat the oven to 180°C | 350°F | Gas 4. Bake the torte for 10–15 minutes, until the ice cream has started to soften. Dust with icing sugar and serve in wedges.

COOK'S TIP *The crumble mixture and pastry can be made without a food processor if you do not have one. Simply rub the butter into the flour and baking powder, then stir in the sugar. To make the pastry, simply stir the additional ingredients into the remaining crumble mixture and bring together with your fingers to make a dough.*

Orange Crêpes with Mascarpone Cream

Baking these delicate crêpes does not actually make them hot when served. Quite simply, the water ice and mascarpone start to melt together in their crisp pancake cases to make a delicious dessert that is neither too rich nor too sweet.

SERVES EIGHT

INGREDIENTS

For the crêpes

115g | 4oz | 1 cup PLAIN (ALL-PURPOSE) FLOUR

300ml | ½ pint | 1¼ cups MILK

1 EGG, plus 1 EGG YOLK

finely grated rind of 1 ORANGE

30ml | 2 tbsp CASTER (SUPERFINE) SUGAR

OIL, for frying

To finish

250g | 9oz | generous 1 cup MASCARPONE CHEESE

15ml | 1 tbsp ICING (CONFECTIONERS') SUGAR

90ml | 6 tbsp SINGLE (LIGHT) CREAM

45ml | 3 tbsp COINTREAU or ORANGE JUICE

500ml | 17fl oz | 2¼ cups ORANGE SORBET (SHERBET)

ICING (CONFECTIONERS') SUGAR, for dusting

1 Make the crêpes. Put the flour, milk, egg and egg yolk, orange rind and sugar in a food processor and blend until smooth. Pour the batter into a jug and leave to stand for 30 minutes.

2 Heat a little of the oil in a medium frying pan or crêpe pan until very hot. Drain off the excess. Pour a little of the batter into the pan, tilting it so that the batter coats the base thinly. Pour any excess back into the jug.

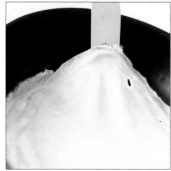

3 Cook the crêpe until the underside is golden, then flip it over with a metal spatula and cook the other side. Slide the crêpe on to a plate and cook seven more crêpes, lightly oiling the pan each time and stacking the cooked ones.

4 Preheat the oven to 200°C | 400°F | Gas 6. In a bowl, beat the mascarpone with the icing sugar, cream and Cointreau or orange juice until smooth. Spread the mixture on the crêpes, taking it almost to the edges.

5 Using a dessertspoon, scoop shavings of sorbet and arrange them to one side of each topped crêpe. Fold the crêpes in half and dust with icing sugar. Fold again into quarters and dust with more icing sugar. Lay the crêpes in a large shallow baking dish and bake for 2 minutes until the sorbet starts to melt. Serve immediately.

elegant iced
desserts

Presentation plays just as important a role
with ice creams as it does with any other
dessert. Whether scooped into glasses and
bathed in a sweet glossy sauce, or cleverly
contained in a chocolate case, there is a
dessert here to suit the mood
of every occasion.

White Chocolate Castles

These impressive chocolate cases serve a wide variety of uses. They can be frozen with iced mousses or other desserts set in them, or, as in this recipe, filled with scoops of ice cream and succulent fresh blueberries.

SERVES SIX

INGREDIENTS

225g | 8oz WHITE CHOCOLATE, broken into pieces

250ml | 8fl oz | 1 cup WHITE CHOCOLATE ICE CREAM

250ml | 8fl oz | 1 cup DARK CHOCOLATE ICE CREAM

115g | 4oz | 1 cup BLUEBERRIES

COCOA POWDER (UNSWEETENED) or ICING (CONFECTIONERS') SUGAR for dusting

1 Put the white chocolate in a heatproof bowl, set it over a pan of gently simmering water and leave until melted. Line a baking sheet with greaseproof (waxed) paper. Cut out six 30 x 13cm | 12 x 5in strips of greaseproof paper, then fold each in half lengthways.

2 Stand a 7.5cm | 3in plain pastry cutter on the baking sheet. Roll one strip of paper into a circle and fit inside the cutter with the folded edge on the base paper. Secure the edges with sticky tape.

3 Remove the cutter and shape the other five paper collars in the same way, leaving the pastry cutter in place around the final collar.

4 Spoon a little of the melted chocolate into the base of the collar supported by the cutter. Using a teaspoon, spread the chocolate over the base and up the sides of the collar, making the top edge uneven. Carefully lift away the cutter.

5 Make five more chocolate cases in the same way, using the cutter for extra support each time. Leave the cases in a cool place or in the refrigerator to set.

6 Carefully peel away the paper from the sides of the chocolate cases then lift the cases off the base. Transfer to serving plates.

7 Using a large melon baller or teaspoon, scoop the white and dark chocolate ice creams into the cases and decorate with the fruit. Dust with cocoa powder or icing sugar and serve at once.

COOK'S TIP *To store the chocolate cases for up to three days, put them in an airtight container and keep in a cool place.*

Water Ice in an Ice Bowl

Nothing sets off a freshly scooped sorbet or sherbet quite so effectively as an ice bowl inlaid with fresh flowers and leaves. Ice bowls are easy to make, inexpensive and stunning enough to grace any special celebration, from a lunch party to a country wedding.

4 Place some kitchen weights or food cans in the central bowl to stop it from rising, then fill the space between the bowls to the rim with more water. Freeze overnight until frozen.

5 Release the inner bowl by pouring boiling water into it almost to the top. Quickly tip out the water and lift away the inner bowl. If the bowl won't come free instantly, repeat the process.

6 To remove the outer bowl, dip it quickly in a large bowl of very hot water until the ice bowl loosens. Return the ice bowl to the freezer.

7 Shortly before serving, scoop the sorbet into the bowl. Return to the freezer until ready to serve.

SERVES EIGHT TO TEN

INGREDIENTS

ICE CUBES

COLD WATER

selection of FRESH EDIBLE
FLOWERS AND LEAVES

18–20 scoops of SORBET
(SHERBET), to serve

1 Place some ice cubes in the base of a 3.5 litre | 6 pint | 15 cup clear plastic or glass freezerproof bowl. Tuck some flowers and leaves around the ice. Position a smaller bowl so that it rests on the ice cubes, leaving an even space between the two bowls.

2 Pour cold water into the space between the bowls until the water level starts to come up the sides. Freeze for 2–3 hours until frozen.

3 Tuck more flowers and leaves between the two bowls, mixing the flowers and leaves so that they look attractive through the sides of the larger bowl.

COOK'S TIP *Use any edible flowers to decorate the bowl, matching the colours to those of the sorbet. Rose petals or small rose buds look lovely, as do any herb flowers, primulas, primroses, pot marigolds, violets, nasturtiums and pansies. Don't place them too closely or the light won't show through. If the inner bowl does not sit perfectly pack crumpled foil between the top edges of the bowls while freezing the ice in the base. When unmoulding the bowl, the ice may crack, but it won't fall apart.*

Gooseberry–Elderflower Water Ice

A classic combination that makes a really refreshing sorbet. Make it in summer, as a stunning finale for an alfresco meal, or save it for serving after a hearty winter's stew.

SERVES SIX

INGREDIENTS

150g | 5oz | ⅔ cup CASTER (SUPERFINE) SUGAR

175ml | 6fl oz | ¾ cup WATER

10 ELDERFLOWER HEADS

500g | 1¼lb | 4 cups GOOSEBERRIES

200ml | 7fl oz | scant 1 cup APPLE JUICE

a little beaten EGG WHITE, CASTER (SUPERFINE) SUGAR and ELDERFLOWERS, to decorate

1 Put 30ml | 2 tbsp of the sugar in a pan with 30ml | 2 tbsp of the water. Set aside. Mix the remaining sugar and water in a separate, heavy pan. Heat gently, stirring occasionally, until the sugar has dissolved. Bring to the boil and boil for 1 minute, without stirring, to make a syrup.

2 Remove from the heat and add the elderflower heads, pressing them into the syrup with a wooden spoon. Leave to infuse for about 1 hour.

3 Strain the elderflower syrup through a sieve placed over a bowl. Set the syrup aside. Add the gooseberries to the pan containing the reserved sugar and water. Cover and cook very gently for about 5 minutes until the gooseberries have softened.

4 Transfer to a food processor and add the apple juice. Process until smooth, then press through a sieve into a bowl. Leave to cool. Stir in the elderflower syrup. Add a dash of green food colouring, if you wish. Chill.

5 BY HAND: Pour the mixture into a shallow container and freeze until thick, preferably overnight.

USING AN ICE CREAM MAKER: Churn the mixture until it holds its shape. Transfer to a freezerproof container and freeze for several hours or overnight.

6 To decorate the glasses, put a little egg white in a shallow bowl and a thin layer of caster sugar on a flat plate. Dip the rim of each glass in the egg white, then the sugar to coat evenly. Leave to dry. Scoop the water ice carefully into the glasses, decorate with elderflowers and serve.

Cranberry Water Ice in Lace Pancakes

Pretty lace pancakes make a really stunning presentation for sorbets, sherbets and ice creams. The sweet yet tangy cranberry water ice can be made using fresh or frozen cranberries, and the result is an impressive dinner party dessert at any time of the year.

SERVES SIX

INGREDIENTS

500g | 1¼lb | 5 cups CRANBERRIES

225g | 8oz | 1 cup CASTER (SUPERFINE) SUGAR

300ml | ½ pint | 1¼ cups ORANGE JUICE

60ml | 4 tbsp COINTREAU or other ORANGE-FLAVOURED LIQUEUR

ICING (CONFECTIONERS') SUGAR, for dusting

extra CRANBERRIES and LIGHTLY WHIPPED CREAM, to serve

For the pancakes

50g | 2oz | ½ cup PLAIN (ALL-PURPOSE) FLOUR

2.5ml | ½ tsp GROUND GINGER

1 EGG

15ml | 1 tbsp CASTER (SUPERFINE) SUGAR

120ml | 4fl oz | ½ cup MILK

a little OIL, for frying

1 Put the cranberries, sugar and orange juice in a pan; heat gently until the sugar has dissolved. Cover and cook for 5–8 minutes, until the fruit is tender. Cool.

2 Process the mixture in a food processor until smooth. Press through a sieve placed over a bowl to extract the juice. Stir the liqueur into the juice. Chill.

3 BY HAND: Pour into a shallow container; freeze for 3–4 hours, beating twice. Freeze overnight.

USING AN ICE CREAM MAKER: Churn the mixture until the water ice holds its shape. Scrape into a container and freeze overnight.

4 Make the pancakes. Sift the flour and ginger into a bowl. Add the egg, sugar and a little of the milk. Gradually whisk in the remaining milk to make a smooth batter. Heat a little oil in a small frying pan or crêpe pan. Pour off the excess oil and remove the pan from the heat.

5 Using a dessertspoon, drizzle a little of the batter over the base of the hot pan, using a scribbling action to give a lacy effect. (The pancake should be about 14cm | 5½in in diameter.) Return the pan to the heat and cook the mixture gently until the lacy pancake is golden on the underside.

6 Carefully turn it over, and cook for 1 minute more. Slide on to a plate and leave to cool. Make five more pancakes in the same way, lightly oiling the pan each time.

7 To serve, lay a pancake on a serving plate. Arrange several small scoops of the water ice on one side of the pancake. Fold over and dust generously with icing sugar. Scatter with extra cranberries. Serve with whipped cream.

COOK'S TIP *When drizzling the batter into the frying pan, make sure all the lacy edges are connected, otherwise the pancakes will fall apart when you try to turn them.*

Iced Vanilla Brûlées

Freeze these little desserts in ramekins. All you have to do before serving is to sprinkle them with sugar and caramelize the topping.

SERVES SIX

INGREDIENTS

1 VANILLA POD (BEAN)

600ml | 1 pint | 2½ cups FULL CREAM (WHOLE) MILK

50g | 2oz | ¼ cup FLAKED RICE

finely grated rind of 2 LEMONS

150g | 5oz | ¾ cup CASTER (SUPERFINE) SUGAR

300ml | ½ pint | 1¼ cups WHIPPING CREAM

sugared STRAWBERRIES, to serve

1 Split the vanilla pod lengthways with a knife and put it in a saucepan. Pour in the milk and add the rice. Simmer for 8–10 minutes until the rice is turning pulpy.

2 Remove the vanilla pod and scrape out the seeds into the pan. Stir in the lemon rind and 75g | 3oz | 6 tbsp of the sugar. Leave to cool.

3 Stir in the cream and churn the mixture in an ice cream maker. Divide among six 150ml | ¼ pint | ⅔ cup ramekins or heatproof dishes, and freeze for at least 3 hours or until firm. Preheat the grill (broiler). Sprinkle each dish with a thick layer of the remaining sugar.

4 Cook under the preheated grill for about 5 minutes until the sugar has caramelized. Serve with the sugared strawberries.

COOK'S TIP *If you haven't got a vanilla pod, use 5ml | 1 tsp natural vanilla essence (extract) instead.*

Miniature Choc-ices

For summer entertaining, these little chocolate-coated ice creams make a fun alternative to the more familiar after-dinner chocolates.

MAKES ABOUT 25

INGREDIENTS

750ml | 1¼ pints | 3 cups VANILLA, DARK CHOCOLATE or COFFEE ICE CREAM

200g | 7oz PLAIN (SEMISWEET) CHOCOLATE, broken into pieces

25g | 1oz MILK CHOCOLATE, broken into pieces

25g | 1oz | ¼ cup chopped HAZELNUTS, lightly toasted

1 Put a large baking sheet in the freezer for 10 minutes. Using a melon baller, scoop balls of the ice cream and place these on the baking sheet. Freeze for at least 1 hour until firm.

2 Line a second baking sheet with non-stick baking parchment and place in the freezer for 15 minutes. Melt the plain chocolate in a heatproof bowl set over a pan of gently simmering water. Melt the milk chocolate in a separate bowl.

3 Using a metal spatula, transfer the ice cream scoops to the paper-lined sheet. Spoon a little plain chocolate over one scoop so that most of it is coated.

4 Scatter immediately with chopped nuts, before the chocolate sets. Coat half the remaining scoops in the same way, scattering each one with nuts before the chocolate sets. Spoon the remaining plain chocolate over all the remaining scoops.

5 Using a teaspoon, drizzle the milk chocolate over the choc-ices which are not topped with nuts. Freeze again until ready to serve.

COOK'S TIP *If the melted milk chocolate is very runny leave it for a few minutes to thicken up slightly before spooning it over the ice cream scoops. The milk chocolate can be piped on the choc-ices, using a piping bag fitted with a writing nozzle.*

Chocolate Teardrops with Cherry Sauce

These sensational chocolate cases are surprisingly easy to make. Once filled, they freeze well, making them the perfect choice for a special occasion dessert.

SERVES SIX

INGREDIENTS

90g | 3½oz PLAIN (SEMISWEET) CHOCOLATE, broken into pieces

115g | 4oz AMARETTI

300ml | ½ pint | 1¼ cups WHIPPING CREAM

2.5ml | ½ tsp ALMOND ESSENCE

30ml | 2 tbsp ICING (CONFECTIONERS') SUGAR

FRESH CHERRIES, to decorate

For the sauce

2.5ml | ½ tsp CORNFLOUR

75ml | 5 tbsp WATER

225g | 8oz | 2 cups FRESH CHERRIES, stoned and halved

45ml | 3 tbsp CASTER SUGAR

10ml | 2 tsp LEMON JUICE

45ml | 3 tbsp GIN

1 Cut out six Perspex (Plexiglass) strips, each measuring 27 x 3cm | 10½ x 1¼in. Put the chocolate in a heatproof bowl over a pan of simmering water. Allow to melt, then remove from the heat and leave for 5 minutes. Line a baking sheet with greaseproof paper.

2 Coat the underside of a Perspex strip in the chocolate, apart from 1cm | ½in at each end. Try to keep the other side uncoated.

3 Bring the ends of the strip together so that the coated side is on the inside. Hold the ends with a paper clip, then put on the baking sheet to set. Make five more shapes in the same way. Chill until set.

4 Put the amaretti in a plastic bag and crush them with a rolling pin. Pour the cream into a bowl, add the almond essence (extract) and icing sugar and whip until thick but still soft. Fold in the biscuits.

5 Spoon the mixture carefully into the chocolate cases, making sure that the chocolate shape is filled with ice cream up to the rim.

6 Tap the baking sheet gently on the work surface so the filling becomes level. Freeze the filled chocolate cases for at least 3 hours or overnight.

7 Make the sauce. Put the cornflour in a small pan and stir in a little of the water to make a paste. Stir in the remaining water, with the cherries, caster (superfine) sugar and lemon juice. Bring to the boil, stirring until thickened. Remove from the heat and leave to cool. Stir in the gin.

8 To serve, remove the paper clips from the chocolate shapes, then carefully peel away the Perspex. Transfer the shapes to individual dessert plates. Spoon a little sauce on to each plate and decorate with the fresh cherries.

Chocolate Mille-feuille Slice

Although this stunning dessert takes a little time to prepare, the good news is that it can be assembled days in advance ready to impress dinner guests. Simply transfer it to the refrigerator about 30 minutes before serving so that it becomes easier to slice.

SERVES EIGHT

INGREDIENTS

4 EGG YOLKS

10ml | 2 tsp CORNFLOUR (CORNSTARCH)

300ml | ½ pint | 1¼ cups MILK

175ml | 6fl oz | ¾ cup MAPLE SYRUP

250ml | 8fl oz | 1 cup CRÈME FRAÎCHE

115g | 4oz | 1 cup PECAN NUTS, chopped

To finish

200g | 7oz PLAIN (SEMISWEET) CHOCOLATE

300ml | ½ pint | 1¼ cups DOUBLE (HEAVY) CREAM

45ml | 3 tbsp ICING (CONFECTIONERS') SUGAR

lightly toasted PECAN NUTS

1 Whisk the egg yolks in a bowl with the cornflour and a little of the milk until smooth. Pour the remaining milk into a pan, bring to the boil, then pour over the yolk mixture, stirring.

2 Return the mixture to the pan and stir in the maple syrup. Cook gently, stirring until thickened and smooth. Do not boil. Pour into a bowl and cover closely with greaseproof (waxed) paper and leave to cool.

3 BY HAND: Stir the crème fraîche into the cold custard and pour into a shallow container. Freeze for 3–4 hours, beating twice during this time, add the chopped pecan nuts and freeze overnight.

USING AN ICE CREAM MAKER: Churn until thick and creamy, then add the chopped pecan nuts. Scrape into a freezerproof container and freeze overnight.

4 Break 150g | 5oz of the chocolate into pieces and melt in a bowl over a pan of simmering water. On greaseproof (waxed) paper draw four rectangles, each measuring 19 x 12cm | 7½ x 4⅓in. Spoon a quarter of the melted chocolate on to each rectangle and spread to the edges. Leave to set.

5 Pare thin curls from the remaining chocolate using a vegetable peeler. Then whip the cream with the icing sugar until it forms soft peaks. Add a dash of brandy first, if you wish. Peel away the paper from a chocolate rectangle and place it on a flat freezerproof serving plate. Spread a third of the whipped cream on the chocolate, almost to the edges.

6 Using a dessertspoon, shape small scoops of the ice cream and lay these over the cream. Cover with a second chocolate rectangle. Repeat the layering, finishing with chocolate. Scatter with the toasted pecan nuts and chocolate curls. Freeze overnight until firm. If freezing the slice for longer, cover it loosely with foil once it is frozen solid.

7 Transfer the frozen slice to the refrigerator 30 minutes before serving to soften slightly.

COOK'S TIP *It is a good idea to assemble the mille-feuille on the upside-down lid of a rectangular freezer tub. The cover can then be fitted and the dessert frozen. Carefully slide the dessert on to a rectangular plate to serve.*

Hazelnut Cones with Vanilla Ice Cream and Hazelnut Caramel Sauce

Unlike bought ice cream cones, these hazelnut cones not only fulfil a function but taste delicious too! They keep well in an airtight container for several days, but should they start to soften, pop them into a moderate oven for a minute or two.

SERVES EIGHT

INGREDIENTS

90g | 3½oz | scant 1 cup GROUND HAZELNUTS

50g | 2oz | ½ cup PLAIN (ALL-PURPOSE) FLOUR

50g | 2oz | ¼ cup CASTER (SUPERFINE) SUGAR

2 EGGS, lightly beaten

5ml | 1 tsp NATURAL VANILLA ESSENCE (EXTRACT)

15ml | 1 tbsp MILK

For the sauce

75g | 3oz | 6 tbsp CASTER (SUPERFINE) SUGAR

60ml | 4 tbsp WATER

50g | 2oz | ½ cup HAZELNUTS, lightly toasted and roughly chopped

15ml | 1 tbsp LEMON JUICE

25g | 1oz | 2 tbsp UNSALTED (SWEET) BUTTER

about 500ml | 17fl oz | 2¼ cups VANILLA ICE CREAM

1 Preheat the oven to 180°C | 350°F | Gas 4. Line a baking sheet with non-stick baking parchment. Mix the ground hazelnuts, flour and sugar in a bowl. Add the eggs, vanilla essence and milk and mix to a smooth paste.

2 Take a shallow tablespoonful of the mixture and spoon it on to one end of the baking sheet. Add a second spoonful at the opposite end. Using a metal spatula spread each spoonful to a circle about 13cm | 5in in diameter, making sure the paste is spread to an even thickness. Bake the biscuits for about 5 minutes until they start to turn pale gold around the edges.

3 Working quickly, lift a biscuit from the paper and turn it over. Wrap it around a cream horn mould to make a cone shape. Repeat with the other biscuit. As soon as the biscuits become brittle, gently ease the cones away from the moulds. Repeat with the remaining mixture to make eight cones in all.

4 Make the sauce. Heat the sugar and water in a small, heavy pan until the sugar has dissolved. Bring to the boil and boil rapidly, without stirring, until the caramel is a deep golden colour. Immediately place the base of the pan in cold water to prevent the caramel from further cooking. Protecting your hand with an oven glove, add 60ml | 4 tbsp water, standing well back in case the syrup splutters.

5 Add the hazelnuts, lemon juice and butter to the pan and cook gently until the sauce is smooth and glossy. Pour into a small jug.

6 Scoop the vanilla ice cream into the hazelnut cones. Pour over a little sauce and serve immediately.

COOK'S TIP *Getting the biscuits to the right thickness is quite tricky, so treat the first batch as a trial run. If the mixture is spread too thickly the biscuits will be rather soft; if too thin, they will crack when wrapped around the cream horn moulds.*

Iced Coffee Cups

Small, sturdy coffee cups make attractive containers for this richly flavoured ice cream. Alternatively use ramekins or other small freezerproof dishes.

3 Spoon the cornflour into a small, heavy pan. Stir in a little of the hot coffee, mixing well, then add the remaining coffee with the egg yolks and sugar. Cook over a gentle heat, stirring constantly until thickened. Do not boil or the mixture may curdle. Scrape into a clean bowl, cover closely with greaseproof (waxed) paper and leave to cool.

4 Whip the cream with the liqueur and cooled coffee mixture until it forms soft peaks.

5 Spoon the mixture into the coffee cups, tapping them gently to level the surface. Freeze for at least 3 hours.

6 Transfer the coffee cups to the refrigerator about 30 minutes before serving. Top with swirls of lightly whipped cream and dust with drinking chocolate powder.

COOK'S TIP *The number of people this will serve depends on the size of the cups. If they are very small, this quantity will serve at least eight.*

SERVES SIX TO EIGHT

INGREDIENTS

150ml | ¼ pint | ⅔ cup WATER

75ml | 5 tbsp GROUND ESPRESSO COFFEE

5ml | 1 tsp CORNFLOUR (CORNSTARCH)

4 EGG YOLKS

65g | 2½oz | 5 tbsp LIGHT MUSCOVADO (BROWN) SUGAR

300ml | ½ pint | 1¼ cups WHIPPING CREAM

30ml | 2 tbsp TIA MARIA or KAHLÚA LIQUEUR

lightly whipped CREAM and DRINKING CHOCOLATE POWDER, to decorate

1 Pour the water into a small pan and stir in the coffee powder. Bring to the boil, remove from the heat and leave to infuse for 15 minutes.

2 Strain through a muslin-lined sieve held over a bowl.

Chocolate Ice Cream in Florentine Baskets

A similar mixture to that used when making florentines is perfect for shaping fluted baskets for holding scoops

of ice cream. For convenience, make the baskets a couple of days in advance, but dip the

edges in chocolate on the day you serve them.

SERVES EIGHT

INGREDIENTS

115g | 4oz | ½ cup UNSALTED
(SWEET) BUTTER

50g | 2oz | ¼ cup CASTER
(SUPERFINE) SUGAR

90ml | 6 tbsp GOLDEN
(LIGHT CORN) SYRUP

90g | 3½oz | scant 1 cup
PLAIN (ALL-PURPOSE) FLOUR

50g | 2oz | ½ cup
FLAKED (SLICED) ALMONDS

50g | 2oz | ¼ cup GLACÉ (CANDIED)
CHERRIES, finely chopped

25g | 1oz | 3 tbsp RAISINS, chopped

15ml | 1 tbsp finely chopped
STEM (CRYSTALLIZED) GINGER

90g | 3½oz PLAIN (SEMISWEET)
CHOCOLATE, broken into pieces

about 750ml | 1¼ pints | 3 cups
DARK CHOCOLATE
ICE CREAM

1 Preheat the oven to 190°C | 375°F | Gas 5. Line two baking sheets with greased non-stick baking parchment. In a small, heavy pan, melt the butter then add the sugar and syrup. Off the heat, stir in the flour, almonds, cherries, raisins and ginger.

2 Place a shallow tablespoonful of the mixture at either end of one baking sheet, then spread each spoonful to a 13cm | 5in round, using the back of the spoon.

3 Bake for about 5 minutes until each round has spread even more and looks lacy and deep golden. Meanwhile spread more circles on the second baking sheet ready to put in the oven. Have ready several metal dariole moulds for shaping the baskets.

4 Leave the biscuits on the baking sheet for about 2 minutes to firm up slightly. Working quickly, lift one biscuit on a fish slice and lay it over an upturned dariole mould. Gently shape the biscuit into flutes around the sides of the mould. Shape the other biscuit around a mould in the same way.

5 Leave the biscuits in place for about 2 minutes until cool, then carefully lift the baskets away from the dariole moulds. Cook and shape the remaining biscuit mixture in the same way until you have eight baskets in total.

6 Melt the chocolate in a heatproof bowl set over a pan of gently simmering water. Carefully dip the edges of the baskets in the melted chocolate and place on individual dessert plates. Scoop the chocolate ice cream into the baskets to serve.

COOK'S TIP *If the biscuits feel as though they are going to fall apart when you lift them from the baking sheet, leave them a little longer to firm up slightly. If they become brittle before you've had a chance to shape them, pop them back in the oven for a few moments to soften.*

Blackcurrant and Meringue Trifles

These quick and easy desserts, made using crushed meringues, cream and water ice, are suitable for any occasion. Leave out the mint if you prefer.

SERVES SIX

INGREDIENTS

350ml | 12fl oz | 1½ cups BLACKCURRANT SORBET

3 bought MERINGUES

several sprigs of MINT

30ml | 2 tbsp ICING SUGAR

20ml | 4 tsp LEMON JUICE

300ml | ½ pint | 1¼ cups DOUBLE (HEAVY) or WHIPPING CREAM

90ml | 6 tbsp GREEK (US STRAINED PLAIN) YOGURT

1 Remove the sorbet (sherbet) from the freezer. Roughly break the meringues into small pieces. Chop the mint and put into a bowl.

2 Add the icing (confectioners') sugar, lemon juice and cream. Whip until the mixture just holds its shape. Stir in the yogurt, then fold in the crushed meringues.

3 Spoon a little of the cream mixture into small, deep dishes or glasses. Add layers of sorbet and cream mixture, ending with cream mixture. Decorate with mint sprigs.

COOK'S TIP *The amount this will serve will depend on the size of the dishes used. If you opt for large bowl-shaped glasses, the mixture will probably serve four.*

Fig, Port and Clementine Sundaes

SERVES SIX

INGREDIENTS

6 CLEMENTINES

30ml | 2 tbsp CLEAR HONEY

1 CINNAMON STICK, halved

15ml | 1 tbsp LIGHT MUSCOVADO (BROWN) SUGAR

60ml | 4 tbsp PORT

6 FRESH FIGS

approx 500ml | 17fl oz | 2¼ cups ORANGE SORBET (SHERBET)

The flavours of figs, cinnamon, clementines and port conjure up images of winter and hearty meals.

1 Finely grate the rind from two clementines and put it in a small, heavy pan. Using a small, sharp knife cut the peel away from all the clementines, then slice the flesh thinly. Add the honey, cinnamon, sugar and port to the clementine rind. Heat gently until the sugar has dissolved, to make a syrup.

2 Put the clementine slices in a heatproof bowl and pour over the syrup. Cool completely, then chill.

3 Slice the figs thinly and add to the clementines and syrup, tossing the ingredients together gently. Leave for 10 minutes, then discard the cinnamon stick.

4 Arrange half the fig and clementine slices around the sides of six serving glasses. Half fill the glasses with scoops of sorbet. Arrange the remaining fruit slices around the sides of the glasses, then pile more sorbet into the centre. Pour over the port syrup and serve.

Iced Raspberry and Almond Trifle

This delicious combination of almond-flavoured sponge, sherried fruit, ice cream and mascarpone topping is sheer indulgence for trifle lovers. The sponge and topping can be made a day in advance and the assembled trifle will sit happily in the refrigerator for an hour before serving.

SERVES EIGHT TO TEN

INGREDIENTS

For the sponge

115g | 4oz | ½ cup UNSALTED (SWEET) BUTTER, softened

115g | 4oz | ½ cup LIGHT MUSCOVADO (BROWN) SUGAR

2 EGGS

75g | 3oz | ⅔ cup SELF-RAISING (SELF-RISING) FLOUR

2.5ml | ½ tsp BAKING POWDER

115g | 4oz | 1 cup GROUND ALMONDS

5ml | 1 tsp ALMOND ESSENCE (EXTRACT)

15ml | 1 tbsp MILK

To finish

300g | 11oz | scant 2 cups RASPBERRIES

50g | 2oz | ½ cup FLAKED (SLICED) ALMONDS, toasted

90ml | 6 tbsp FRESH ORANGE JUICE

200ml | 7fl oz | scant 1 cup MEDIUM SHERRY

500g | 1¼lb | 2½ cups MASCARPONE CHEESE

150g | 5oz | ⅔ cup GREEK (US STRAINED PLAIN) YOGURT

30ml | 2 tbsp ICING (CONFECTIONERS') SUGAR

about 250ml | 8fl oz | 1 cup VANILLA ICE CREAM

about 250ml | 8fl oz | 1 cup RASPBERRY ICE CREAM

1 Preheat the oven to 180°C | 350°F | Gas 4. Grease and line a 20cm | 8in round cake tin (pan). Put the butter, sugar, eggs, flour, baking powder, almonds and almond essence in a large bowl and beat with an electric whisk for 2 minutes until creamy. Stir in the milk.

2 Spoon the mixture into the prepared tin, level the surface and bake for about 30 minutes or until just firm in the centre. Transfer to a wire rack and leave to cool.

3 Cut the sponge into chunky pieces and place these in the base of a 1.75 litre | 3 pint | 7½ cup glass serving dish. Scatter with half the raspberries and almonds. Mix the orange juice with 90ml | 6 tbsp of the sherry.

4 Spoon over the orange and sherry mixture. Beat the mascarpone in a bowl with the yogurt, icing sugar and remaining sherry. Put the trifle dish and the mascarpone mixture in the refrigerator until you are ready to assemble the trifle.

5 To serve, scoop the ice cream and sorbet into the trifle dish. Reserve a few of the remaining raspberries and almonds for the decoration, then scatter the rest over the ice cream. Spoon over the mascarpone mixture and scatter with the reserved raspberries and almonds. Chill the trifle for up to 1 hour before serving.

COOK'S TIP *The trifle will set better if all the ingredients are thoroughly chilled in the refrigerator before assembling. Chill again before serving.*

VARIATION *There are many variations on this recipe that work equally well. Try any other soft summer fruits or tropical fruits and complementary ice creams or sorbets.*

Pear and Gingerbread Sundaes

The best sundaes do not consist solely of ice cream, but are a feast of flavours that melt

into each other, rather like a trifle. Poach the pears and chill them well in advance,

so that the dessert can be assembled in minutes.

SERVES FOUR

INGREDIENTS

65g | 2½oz | ⅓ cup LIGHT
MUSCOVADO (BROWN) SUGAR

90ml | 6 tbsp WATER

30ml | 2 tbsp LEMON JUICE

40g | 1½oz | ¼ cup
SULTANAS (GOLDEN RAISINS)

1.5ml | ¼ tsp
MIXED (APPLE PIE) SPICE

4 SMALL PEARS

150g | 5oz MOIST GINGERBREAD
or GINGER CAKE

250ml | 8fl oz | 1 cup
VANILLA ICE CREAM

1 Heat the sugar and water in a heavy pan until the sugar has dissolved. Add the lemon juice, dried fruit and spice. Peel, quarter and core the pears and add them to the pan.

2 Cover and simmer very gently for 5–10 minutes until just tender. Cool the pears in the syrup. Lift them out of the syrup and put them in a bowl. Pour the syrup into a jug. Chill both.

3 Cut the gingerbread or ginger cake into four pieces and arrange in four serving glasses. Divide the pears among the glasses, then pile ice cream in the centre of each portion. Pour a little of the syrup over each sundae and serve.

VARIATION *This quick and easy dessert can be made just as successfully with tart dessert apples.*

Coconut Ice Cream with Mango Sauce

Halved coconut shells make impressive serving containers for this rich and delicious

ice cream. You'll need to crack open three coconuts to get six serving cups,

plus enough trimmings to use in the ice cream.

SERVES SIX

INGREDIENTS

4 EGG YOLKS

115g | 4oz | ½ cup CASTER
(SUPERFINE) SUGAR

15ml | 1 tbsp CORNFLOUR
(CORNSTARCH)

5ml | 1 tsp ALMOND ESSENCE

600ml | 1 pint | 2½ cups MILK

150g | 5oz | 1½ cups FRESHLY
GRATED COCONUT, or GRATED
CREAMED COCONUT

300ml | ½ pint | 1¼ cups
WHIPPING CREAM

For the sauce

1 LARGE RIPE MANGO

30ml | 2 tbsp CASTER SUGAR

15ml | 1 tbsp LEMON JUICE

60ml | 4 tbsp FRESH ORANGE JUICE

1 Beat the egg yolks, sugar, cornflour, almond essence (extract) and a little of the milk until combined. If using freshly grated coconut, process with 300ml | ½ pint | 1¼ cups of the milk until fairly smooth.

2 Pour the coconut milk into a heavy pan and stir in the rest of the milk. For creamed coconut, heat it with the milk, stirring. Bring the milk almost to the boil.

3 Gradually pour the milk over the egg yolks, whisking constantly. Return the mixture to the pan and cook very gently, stirring until thickened. Pour the custard into a bowl, cover with greaseproof (waxed) paper and leave to cool.

4 BY HAND: Whip the cream and fold into the custard. Transfer to a freezer container and freeze for 3–4 hours, beating twice as it thickens. Freeze again overnight.

USING AN ICE CREAM MAKER: Stir in the cream and churn until it holds its shape. Spoon into a freezer container and freeze for several hours or overnight.

5 To make the sauce, slice the mango flesh off the stone and put it into a food processor. Add the sugar, lemon juice and orange juice and process until smooth. Pour into a small jug and chill.

6 To serve, scoop the prepared ice cream into the halved coconut shells, or into tall serving glasses. Add the chilled mango sauce and serve immediately.

ice creams

with fruit

Whether served as an accompaniment or churned into ice cream or water ice, an abundance of tangy fruit gives a light, fresh taste. For an invigorating summer cooler or a finale to a rich meal, fruit ices make a vibrant marriage of colour and flavour.

Passion Fruit Mousses

Passion fruit has an exotic, tangy flavour that works wonderfully well in a creamy mousse. The raised paper collar is one of the tricks of the trade – peel it away and the texture and sophisticated shape of the mousse are revealed.

SERVES SIX

INGREDIENTS

9 ripe PASSION FRUIT

10ml | 2 tsp POWDERED GELATINE

45ml | 3 tbsp WATER

3 EGGS, separated

75g | 3oz | 6 tbsp CASTER (SUPERFINE) SUGAR

30ml | 2 tbsp LEMON JUICE

250ml | 8fl oz | 1 cup DOUBLE (HEAVY) or WHIPPING CREAM

1 Cut out six 30 x 7.5cm | 12 x 3in strips of non-stick baking parchment. Wrap each strip around a 150ml | ¼ pint | ⅔ cup ramekin, holding it in place with a paper clip. Secure with string under the rim of each paper collar.

2 Cut the passion fruit in half and use a teaspoon to scoop the pulp into a sieve set over a bowl. Press the pulp in the sieve with the back of a large spoon to extract as much juice as possible.

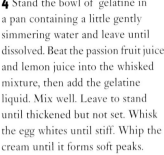

3 Sprinkle the gelatine over the water in a small, heatproof bowl and leave to soak for 5 minutes or until spongy. Whisk the egg yolks and sugar in a bowl until the mixture is pale and creamy.

4 Stand the bowl of gelatine in a pan containing a little gently simmering water and leave until dissolved. Beat the passion fruit juice and lemon juice into the whisked mixture, then add the gelatine liquid. Mix well. Leave to stand until thickened but not set. Whisk the egg whites until stiff. Whip the cream until it forms soft peaks.

5 Using a large metal spoon, fold the cream into the yolk mixture. Stir in a quarter of the egg whites to loosen the mixture, then fold in the remainder. Spoon into the prepared dishes so that the mixture comes well above the rim of each dish. Freeze the mousses for at least 4 hours.

6 About 30 minutes before you intend to serve them, gently peel away the paper collars from the mousses and transfer them to the refrigerator to soften slightly.

COOK'S TIP *Before filling the ramekins, stand them on a small baking sheet. That way, you can transfer them all to the freezer in one go.*

Iced Summer Pudding

SERVES SIX TO EIGHT

This is a frozen version of the classic and ever-popular soft-fruit dessert. Made using good quality fruit water ice and strawberry or raspberry ice cream, the result is just as delicious and looks very impressive.

INGREDIENTS

25g | 1 oz | 2 tbsp
CASTER (SUPERFINE) SUGAR

60ml | 4 tbsp WATER

75ml | 5 tbsp
STRAWBERRY JAM

60ml | 4 tbsp
CRÈME DE CASSIS

225g | 8oz | 2 cups
SMALL STRAWBERRIES,
thinly sliced

250g | 9oz GOOD QUALITY
MADEIRA CAKE

250ml | 8fl oz | 1 cup
SOFT FRUIT SORBET (SHERBET)

500ml | 17fl oz | 2¼ cups
STRAWBERRY
or RASPBERRY
ICE CREAM

1 Line a 1.5 litre | 2½ pint | 6¼ cup ovenproof bowl with clear film (plastic wrap). Heat the sugar and water in a small, heavy pan until the sugar has dissolved.

2 Meanwhile, press 30ml | 2 tbsp of the strawberry jam through a sieve into a small bowl. Stir in 15ml | 1 tbsp of the syrup and brush the mixture up the sides of the lined basin. Press the remaining jam through the sieve into the pan of syrup and stir in the crème de cassis until smooth.

3 Press the strawberry slices in a single layer over the base and sides of the basin, fitting them as tightly together as possible. Chill. Cut the cake into 1cm | ½in slices.

4 Dip the cake slices in the remaining syrup and arrange in a single layer over the strawberries, cutting the sponge to fit and trimming off the excess around the edges. Freeze for 30 minutes.

5 Remove the sorbet from the freezer to soften for about 15 minutes. Using a large metal spoon, pack the sorbet into the basin – it will fill it about three-quarters full – and level the surface. Return the basin to the freezer for 30 minutes. Remove the ice cream from the freezer for about 15 minutes to soften.

6 Pack the ice cream over the sorbet, filling the basin. Level the surface and freeze for at least 4 hours or overnight.

7 To serve, dip the bowl in very hot water for 2 seconds then invert the iced pudding on to a serving plate. Peel away the clear film and serve the pudding in wedges.

COOK'S TIP *Any soft fruit sorbet can be used. Raspberry sorbet has a wonderfully intense colour; blackcurrant or redcurrant sorbet would also be excellent choices.*

Peach Mousse Cakes

These light and airy frozen mousses, sandwiched between layers of whisked sponge, can be made ahead for a dinner party dessert or thawed and served for a special tea. You will need a couple of sheets of flexible Perspex for shaping the moulds.

MAKES EIGHT

INGREDIENTS

For the sponge

3 EGGS

75g | 3oz | 6 tbsp CASTER (SUPERFINE) SUGAR

75g | 3oz | ⅔ cup PLAIN (ALL-PURPOSE) FLOUR

For the mousse

10ml | 2 tsp POWDERED GELATINE

45ml | 3 tbsp WATER

6 RIPE PEACHES

finely grated rind of 1 ORANGE

75g | 3oz | 6 tbsp CASTER (SUPERFINE) SUGAR

2 EGG WHITES

150ml | ¼ pint | ⅔ cup DOUBLE (HEAVY) CREAM

45ml | 3 tbsp COINTREAU or other ORANGE-FLAVOURED LIQUEUR

COOK'S TIP *There are two main types of peaches: "freestone" and "clingstone". As the name suggests, the stone of the "freestone" type separates more easily from the flesh and is therefore better for using in this dish.*

1 Preheat the oven to 180°C | 350°F | Gas 4. Grease a 33 x 23cm | 13 x 9in Swiss roll tin and line with greaseproof (waxed) paper. Grease the paper. Put the eggs and sugar in a heatproof bowl, place over a pan of gently simmering water and whisk until the mixture forms a trail when the whisk is lifted from the bowl. Remove from the heat and whisk for 2 minutes until cool.

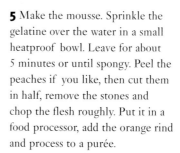

2 Sift the flour into the bowl and fold in, using a large metal spoon. Scrape into the prepared tin, gently spreading the mixture into the corners. Bake for about 15 minutes until just firm. Leave to cool. Cut out eight 25 x 5cm | 10 x 2in strips of Perspex.

3 Using a 7.5cm | 3in biscuit cutter, cut out eight circles from the sponge. Carefully slice each round horizontally in half. Roll a piece of Perspex (Plexiglass) into a round and fit it around one of the pieces of sponge, making sure the sponge is cut side up, so that the sponge fits snugly in its Perspex collar.

4 Secure the Perspex with tape. Make seven more sponge-based cases in the same way and place them on a small tray.

5 Make the mousse. Sprinkle the gelatine over the water in a small heatproof bowl. Leave for about 5 minutes or until spongy. Peel the peaches if you like, then cut them in half, remove the stones and chop the flesh roughly. Put it in a food processor, add the orange rind and process to a purée.

6 Put about a quarter of the purée in a small pan with the sugar and soaked gelatine; heat until both sugar and gelatine have dissolved. Beat the mixture into the remaining purée. Leave until thickened but not set.

7 Whisk the egg whites in a clean, grease-free bowl until stiff. Whip the cream with the liqueur until soft peaks start to form. Using a large metal spoon, carefully fold the cream into the purée, followed by the egg whites.

8 Divide the mousse mixture evenly among the sponge-filled cases and gently level the tops.

9 Position the remaining sponge rounds over the filling, making sure the uncut sides of the sponges are uppermost. Press down gently. Freeze for at least 3 hours.

10 To serve, dust the tops of the cakes with a little icing sugar, then gently peel away the Perspex.

Lemon Ice Cups with Summer Fruits

In this stunning dessert, lemon sorbet or sherbet is moulded into cup shapes to make pretty containers for a selection of summer fruits. Other combinations, such as mango cups for tropical fruits, or orange cups for blueberries, also work well.

SERVES SIX

INGREDIENTS

500ml | 17fl oz | 2¼ cups
LEMON SORBET (SHERBET)

225g | 8oz | 2 cups SMALL
STRAWBERRIES

150g | 5oz | scant 1 cup
RASPBERRIES

75g | 3oz | ¾ cup REDCURRANTS,
BLACKCURRANTS or
WHITECURRANTS

15ml | 1 tbsp CASTER
(SUPERFINE) SUGAR

45ml | 3 tbsp COINTREAU

1 Put six 150ml | ¼ pint | ⅔ cup metal moulds in the freezer for 15 minutes to chill. At the same time, remove the sorbet from the freezer to soften slightly.

2 Using a teaspoon, pack the sorbet into the moulds, building up a layer about 1cm | ½in thick around the base and sides, and leaving a deep cavity in the centre. Hold each mould in a dish towel as you work (see Cook's Tip). Return each mould to the freezer when it is lined.

3 Cut the strawberries in half and place in a bowl with the raspberries and red, black or whitecurrants. Add the sugar and liqueur and toss the ingredients together lightly. Cover and chill for at least 2 hours.

4 Once the sorbet in the moulds has frozen completely, loosen the edges with a knife, then dip in a bowl of very hot water for 2 seconds. Invert the sorbet cups on to a tray, using a fork to twist and loosen the cups if necessary.

5 If you need to, dip the moulds very briefly in the hot water again. Turn the cups over so they are ready to fill and return to the freezer until required.

6 To serve, place the cups on serving plates and fill with the fruits, spooning over any juices.

COOK'S TIP *When lining a metal mould with the lemon sorbet it is a good idea to wrap your hand in a dishtowel. This not only prevents your fingers from sticking to the metal, but also stops the heat from your hands from warming the mould.*

Spiced Ice Pears

Pears poached in wine make an elegant dessert at any time of the year. In this recipe the pears are hollowed out and filled with a wine-and-pear flavoured sorbet.

5 Cut a 2.5cm | 1in slice off the top of each pear and reserve. Use an apple corer to remove the cores.

6 Using a teaspoon, scoop out the centre of each pear, leaving a thick shell. Put the scooped-out flesh in a food processor or blender and the hollowed pears and their lids in the freezer. Strain the poaching juices. Set 75ml | 5 tbsp aside for serving and add the rest to the food processor. Blend until smooth.

7 BY HAND: Pour the mixture into a container and freeze for 3–4 hours, beating twice as it thickens.

USING AN ICE CREAM MAKER:
Churn the mixture in an ice cream maker until it holds its shape.

Using a teaspoon, pack the sorbet into the frozen pears, piling it up high. Position the lids and return to the freezer overnight.

8 Remove the pears from the freezer and let them stand at room temperature about 30 minutes before serving. The pears should have softened but the sorbet remains icy. Transfer to serving plates and spoon a little of the reserved syrup around each one.

SERVES SIX

INGREDIENTS

600ml | 1 pint | 2½ cups
RED WINE

2 CINNAMON STICKS

115g | 4oz | generous ½ cup
CASTER (SUPERFINE) SUGAR

6 PLUMP PEARS

1 Put the wine, halved cinnamon sticks and sugar in a heavy pan, that is big enough for the pears. Heat gently to dissolve the sugar.

2 Peel the pears, leaving the stalks attached. Stand them upright in the syrup in the saucepan, taking care not to pack them too tightly.

3 Cover and simmer very gently for 10–20 minutes until just tender, turning so they colour evenly. (The cooking time varies depending on the softness of the pears.)

4 Lift out the pears with a slotted spoon and set them aside to cool. Boil the juices briefly until reduced to 350ml | 12fl oz | 1½ cups. Set aside and leave to cool.

Iced Melon with Pimm's

Freezing sorbet or sherbet in hollowed-out fruit, which is then cut into icy wedges, is an excellent idea. The novel presentation and refreshing flavour make this dessert irresistible on a hot summer's afternoon. The idea works particularly well with melon wedges, laced with chilled Pimm's.

SERVES SIX

INGREDIENTS

50g | 2oz | ¼ cup CASTER (SUPERFINE) SUGAR

30ml | 2 tbsp CLEAR HONEY

15ml | 1 tbsp LEMON JUICE

60ml | 4 tbsp WATER

1 medium CANTALOUPE or CHARENTAIS MELON, about 1 kg | 2¼lb

CRUSHED ICE, CUCUMBER SLICES and BORAGE LEAVES, to decorate

PIMM'S NO. 1, to decorate

1 Put the sugar, honey, lemon juice and water in a small heavy pan and heat gently until the sugar dissolves. Bring to the boil and boil for 1 minute, without stirring, to make a syrup. Leave to cool.

2 Cut the melon in half and discard the seeds. Carefully scoop out the flesh and place into a food processor, taking care to keep the shells intact.

3 Blend the melon flesh until smooth. Then transfer to a bowl, stir in the cooled syrup and chill in the refrigerator until very cold. Invert the melon shells and leave them to drain on kitchen paper, then transfer to the freezer while making the sorbet.

4 BY HAND: Pour the mixture into a container and freeze for 3–4 hours, beating twice with a fork, a whisk or in a food processor, to break up the ice crystals.

USING AN ICE CREAM MAKER: Churn the melon mixture in an ice cream maker until the sorbet holds its shape.

5 Pack the sorbet into the melon shells and level the surface with a knife. Then use a dessertspoon to scoop out the centre of each filled melon shell to simulate the seed cavity. Freeze overnight until firm.

6 To serve, use a large knife to cut each half into three wedges. Serve on a bed of crushed ice on a large platter or individual serving plates, and decorate with the cucumber slices and borage. Drizzle lightly with Pimm's.

COOK'S TIP *If the melon sorbet is too firm to cut when taken straight from the freezer, let it soften in the refrigerator slightly. Take care when slicing the frozen melon shell into wedges. A serrated kitchen knife is easiest to use.*

Iced Clementines

*These pretty, filled fruits store well in the freezer, and will prove perfect for an impromptu summer party, an **al fresco** meal or simply a refreshing treat on a hot summer's afternoon.*

MAKES 12

INGREDIENTS

16 LARGE CLEMENTINES

175g | 6oz | scant 1 cup CASTER (SUPERFINE) SUGAR

105ml | 7 tbsp WATER

juice of 2 LEMONS

a little FRESH ORANGE JUICE (if necessary)

FRESH MINT or LEMON BALM LEAVES, to decorate

1 Slice the tops off 12 of the clementines to make lids. Set aside on a baking sheet. Loosen the clementine flesh with a sharp knife then carefully scoop it out into a bowl, keeping the shells intact. Scrape out as much of the membrane from the shells as possible. Add the shells to the lids and put them in the freezer.

2 Put the sugar and water in a heavy pan and heat gently, stirring until the sugar dissolves. Boil for 3 minutes without stirring, then leave the syrup to cool. Stir in the lemon juice.

3 Finely grate the rind from the remaining clementines. Squeeze the fruits and add the juice and rind to the syrup.

4 Process the clementine flesh in a food processor or blender, then press it through a sieve placed over a bowl to extract as much juice as possible. Add this to the syrup. You need about 900ml | 1½ pints | 3¾ cups of liquid. Make up with fresh orange juice if necessary.

5 BY HAND: Pour the mixture into a shallow container and freeze for 3–4 hours, beating twice as the sorbet thickens.

USING AN ICE CREAM MAKER: Churn the mixture until it holds its shape.

Pack the sorbet into the empty clementine shells, mounding them up slightly in the centre. Position the lids and return to the freezer for several hours or overnight.

6 Transfer the clementines to the refrigerator about 30 minutes before serving, to soften. Serve on individual plates and decorate.

Peach and Almond Granita

Infused almonds make a richly flavoured "milk" that forms the basis of this light, tangy dessert, which would be the ideal choice to follow a rich main course.

3 Add the caster sugar and almond essence to the pan, with half the lemon juice and the remaining water. Heat gently until the sugar dissolves, then bring to the boil. Lower the heat and simmer gently for 3 minutes without stirring, taking care that the syrup does not boil over. Remove from the heat and leave to cool.

4 Cut the peaches in half and remove the stones. Using a small knife, scoop out about half the flesh to enlarge the cavities. Put the flesh in a food processor. Brush the exposed flesh with the remaining lemon juice and chill the peaches until required.

5 Add the almond syrup to the peach flesh and process until smooth. Pour into a shallow freezer container and freeze until ice crystals have formed around the edges. Stir with a fork, then freeze again until more crystals have formed around the edges. Repeat until the mixture has the consistency of crushed ice.

6 Lightly break up the granita with a fork to loosen the mixture. Spoon into the peach halves and serve two on each plate. Drizzle a little Amaretto liqueur over the top, if using.

COOK'S TIP *The scooped peach shells will keep overnight in the refrigerator if you brush them with lemon juice and wrap them in clear film.*
If you want to make the granita further ahead, simply use the flesh of three peaches and serve in tall glasses.

SERVES SIX

INGREDIENTS

115g | 4oz | 1 cup GROUND ALMONDS

900ml | 1½ pints | 3¾ cups WATER

150g | 5oz | ¾ cup CASTER (SUPERFINE) SUGAR

5ml | 1 tsp ALMOND ESSENCE (EXTRACT)

juice of 2 LEMONS

6 PEACHES

DISARONNO AMARETTO LIQUEUR, to serve (optional)

1 Put the ground almonds in a saucepan and pour in 600ml | 1 pint | 2½ cups of the water. Bring just to the boil then lower the heat and simmer gently for 2 minutes. Remove from the heat and leave to stand for 30 minutes.

2 Strain the mixture through a fine sieve placed over a bowl, and press lightly, with the back of a spoon, to extract as much liquid as possible. Pour the liquid into a clean, heavy pan.

Strawberry Semi-freddo

Serve this quick strawberry and ricotta dessert semi-frozen to enjoy the flavour at its best. The contrasting texture of crisp dessert biscuits makes them the perfect accompaniment.

SERVES FOUR TO SIX

INGREDIENTS

250g | 9oz | generous 2 cups
STRAWBERRIES

115g | 4oz | scant ½ cup
STRAWBERRY JAM

250g | 9oz | generous 1 cup
RICOTTA CHEESE

200g | 7oz | scant 1 cup
GREEK (US STRAINED
PLAIN) YOGURT

5ml | 1 tsp VANILLA ESSENCE
(EXTRACT)

40g | 1½oz | 3 tbsp CASTER
(SUPERFINE) SUGAR

1 Put the strawberries in a bowl and mash them with a fork until broken into small pieces but not completely puréed. Stir in the strawberry jam. Drain off any whey from the ricotta cheese.

2 Tip the ricotta cheese into a bowl and stir in the yogurt, natural vanilla essence and sugar. Using a dessertspoon, gently fold the mashed strawberries into the ricotta mixture for a rippled effect.

3 Spoon the mixture into individual freezerproof dishes and freeze for at least 2 hours until almost solid. Alternatively freeze until completely solid, then transfer the ice cream to the refrigerator for about 45 minutes to soften before serving. Serve in small bowls with extra strawberries and decorated with mint or lemon balm.

COOK'S TIP *Don't mash the strawberries too much or they'll become too liquid. Freeze in a large freezer container if you don't have suitable small dishes. Transfer to the refrigerator to thaw slightly, then scoop into glasses.*

herb, spice & flower ices

For those with an adventurous taste in ice cream, here is an intriguing repertoire of less predictable flavours such as Turkish delight, lavender and even chilli. The ices in the following collection are quick and easy to make, and will have everyone guessing the intrinsic flavours.

Rosemary Ice Cream

Fresh rosemary has a lovely fragrance that works as well in sweet dishes as it does in savoury.

Serve this ice cream as an accompaniment to soft fruit or plum compote, or on its own,

with amaretti or other dessert biscuits.

SERVES SIX

INGREDIENTS

300ml | ½ pint | 1¼ cups MILK

4 large
FRESH ROSEMARY
SPRIGS

3 EGG YOLKS

75g | 3oz | 6 tbsp
CASTER (SUPERFINE) SUGAR

10ml | 2 tsp CORNFLOUR
(CORNSTARCH)

400ml | 14fl oz | 1¾ cups
CRÈME FRAÎCHE

about 15ml | 1 tbsp DEMERARA
(RAW) SUGAR

ROSEMARY SPRIGS and HERB
FLOWERS, to decorate

RATAFIA BISCUITS
(ALMOND MACAROONS), to serve

1 Put the milk and rosemary sprigs in a heavy pan. Bring almost to the boil, remove from the heat and leave to infuse for about 20 minutes. Place the egg yolks in a bowl and whisk in the sugar and the cornflour.

2 Return the pan to the heat and bring almost to the boil. Gradually pour into the yolk mixture and stir it in well. Return to the pan and cook over a very gentle heat, stirring constantly until it thickens. Do not let it boil or it may curdle.

3 Strain the custard through a sieve into a bowl. Cover the surface closely with greaseproof (waxed) paper and leave to cool. Chill the custard until it is very cold, then stir in the crème fraîche, mixing well.

4 BY HAND: Pour the mixture into a container and freeze for 3–4 hours, beating twice as it thickens. Return to the freezer until ready to serve.

USING AN ICE CREAM MAKER: Churn the mixture until thick, then scrape it into a tub or similar freezerproof container. Freeze until ready to serve.

5 Transfer the ice cream to the refrigerator 30 minutes before serving to soften slightly. Scoop into dessert dishes, sprinkle with demerara sugar and decorate with fresh rosemary sprigs and herb flowers. Serve with ratafia biscuits.

COOK'S TIP *For a very attractive effect use herb flowers that complement the colour of your dessert dishes.*

Lavender and Honey Ice Cream

Lavender and honey make a memorable partnership in this old-fashioned and elegant ice cream.

Serve scooped into glasses or set in little moulds and top with lightly whipped cream.

Pretty lavender flowers add the finishing touch.

SERVES SIX TO EIGHT

INGREDIENTS

90ml | 6 tbsp CLEAR HONEY

4 EGG YOLKS

10ml | 2 tsp CORNFLOUR (CORNSTARCH)

8 LAVENDER SPRIGS, plus extra to decorate

450ml | ¾ pint | scant 2 cups MILK

450ml | ¾ pint | scant 2 cups WHIPPING CREAM

DESSERT BISCUITS (COOKIES), to serve

1 Put the honey, egg yolk, and cornflour in a bowl. Separate the lavender flowers and add them to the bowl plus a little of the milk. Whisk lightly. In a heavy pan bring the remaining milk just to the boil. Add to the egg yolk mixture, stirring well.

2 Return the mixture to the pan and cook very gently, stirring until the mixture thickens. Pour the custard into a bowl, cover the surface closely with a circle of greaseproof (waxed) paper and leave to cool, then chill in the freezer until very cold.

3 BY HAND: Whip the cream and fold into the custard. Pour into a container and freeze for 3–4 hours, beating twice as it thickens. Return to the freezer until ready to serve.

USING AN ICE CREAM MAKER: Stir the cream into the custard, then churn the mixture until it holds its shape. Transfer to a tub or similar freezerproof container and freeze until ready to serve.

4 Transfer the ice cream to the refrigerator 30 minutes before serving, so that it softens slightly. Scoop into small dishes, decorate with lavender flowers and serve with dessert biscuits.

Basil and Orange Granita

More often associated with savoury dishes, basil has a sweet, aromatic flavour that complements tangy oranges beautifully. This classic combination makes a perfect refresher between courses.

SERVES SIX

INGREDIENTS

5 LARGE ORANGES

175g | 6oz | scant 1 cup
CASTER (SUPERFINE) SUGAR

450ml | ¾ pint | scant 2 cups WATER

ORANGE JUICE (if necessary)

15g | ½oz | ½ cup FRESH
BASIL LEAVES

TINY FRESH BASIL LEAVES,
to decorate

1 Pare the rind thinly from three oranges and place in a pan. Add the sugar and water. Heat gently until the sugar has dissolved. Cool, pour into a bowl and chill.

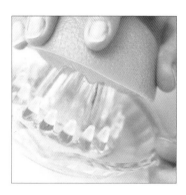

2 Squeeze the juice from all the oranges and pour it into a large measuring jug. You should have about 500ml | 17fl oz | 2¼ cups. Make it up to the required quantity with fresh orange juice if necessary.

3 Pour the juice into a food processor or blender and add the basil leaves. Process the mixture in short bursts until the basil has been chopped into small pieces.

4 Using a slotted spoon, remove the orange rind from the chilled syrup. Stir in the orange juice and basil mixture, then pour into a plastic tub or similar freezerproof container. Cover and freeze for about 2 hours or until the mixture is mushy around the edges. Break up the ice crystals with a fork and stir well.

5 Freeze for 30 minutes more until once again frozen around the edges. Mash with a fork and return to the freezer. Repeat the process until the ice forms fine crystals.

6 To serve, spoon the granita into tall glasses and decorate with tiny fresh basil leaves.

Star Anise and Grapefruit Granita

With its aniseed flavour, star anise makes an interesting addition to many fruit desserts and its dramatic appearance makes it the ideal decoration. This refreshing granita will stand out as it is both tangy and sweet.

SERVES SIX

INGREDIENTS

200g | 7oz | 1 cup
CASTER (SUPERFINE) SUGAR

450ml | ¾ pint | scant 2 cups WATER

6 WHOLE STAR ANISE

4 GRAPEFRUIT

1 Put the sugar and water in a pan and heat gently, stirring every now and then, until the sugar has completely dissolved. Stir in the star anise and heat the syrup gently for 2 minutes, without stirring. Remove from the heat and leave to cool.

2 Take a slice off the top and bottom of each grapefruit, then slice off the skin and pith. Chop the flesh roughly and place it in a food processor. Process until almost smooth, then press the pulp through a sieve into a bowl.

3 Strain the syrup into the bowl, reserving the star anise. Mix well, then pour the mixture into a shallow freezerproof container. Cover and freeze for about 2 hours until the mixture starts to freeze and form ice crystals around the edges of the container.

4 Using a fork, break up the ice crystals, then return the mixture to the freezer. Freeze for 30 minutes more, mash with a fork again, then return to the freezer. Repeat the process until the mixture forms fine ice crystals.

5 To serve, spoon the granita into glasses and decorate with the reserved star anise.

COOK'S TIP *Buy whole star anise from a shop or market that sells spices loose or packaged in clear cellophane. When the spice is packed in boxes, it is often broken into sections and the quality and flavour will have deteriorated.*

Lemon and Cardamom Ice Cream

Combining lemon and cardamom gives this dessert a lovely "clean" tang – ideal after a spicy main course.

SERVES SIX

INGREDIENTS

15ml | 1 tbsp CARDAMOM PODS

4 EGG YOLKS

115g | 4oz CASTER (SUPERFINE) SUGAR

10ml | 2 tsp CORNFLOUR (CORNSTARCH)

grated rind and juice of 3 LEMONS

300ml | ½ pint | 1¼ cups MILK

300ml | ½ pint | 1¼ cups WHIPPING CREAM

FRESH LEMON BALM SPRIGS and ICING SUGAR, to decorate

1 Put the cardamom pods in a mortar and crush them with a pestle to release the seeds. Pick out and discard the shells, then grind the seeds to break them up slightly.

2 Put the egg yolks, caster sugar, cornflour, lemon rind and juice in a bowl. Add the cardamom seeds and whisk well.

3 Bring the milk to the boil in a heavy pan, then pour over the egg yolk mixture, stirring well. Return the mixture to the pan and cook over a very gentle heat, stirring constantly until the custard thickens.

4 Pour the custard into a bowl, cover the surface closely with a circle of greaseproof (waxed) paper and leave to cool. Chill until very cold.

5 BY HAND: Whip the cream lightly and fold into the custard. Pour into a container and freeze for 3–4 hours, beating twice as it thickens. Return to the freezer until required.

USING AN ICE CREAM MAKER: Whisk the cream lightly into the custard and churn the mixture until it holds its shape. Transfer to a container; freeze until needed.

6 Transfer to the refrigerator 30 minutes before serving. Scoop into glasses and decorate with the lemon balm and sugar.

COOK'S TIP *Lemon balm is an easy herb to grow. The leaves are best picked before the flowering period, when they are at their most fragrant.*

Saffron, Apricot and Almond Cream

SERVES SIX TO EIGHT

This vibrant, chunky ice cream has a slightly Middle-Eastern flavour. Although saffron is expensive, its intense colour and distinctive flavour are well worth it, and you only need a small amount.

INGREDIENTS

150g | 5oz | ⅔ cup DRIED APRICOTS

60ml | 4 tbsp COINTREAU

2.5ml | ½ tsp SAFFRON STRANDS, lightly crushed

15ml | 1 tbsp BOILING WATER

3 EGG YOLKS

75g | 3oz | 6 tbsp CASTER (SUPERFINE) SUGAR

10ml | 2 tsp CORNFLOUR (CORNSTARCH)

300ml | ½ pint | 1¼ cups MILK

300ml | ½ pint | 1¼ cups SINGLE (LIGHT) CREAM

75g | 3oz | ¾ cup UNBLANCHED ALMONDS, lightly toasted

AMARETTI, to serve (optional)

1 Chop the apricots into small pieces and put them in a bowl. Add the liqueur and leave for about 1 hour or until absorbed. Put the saffron in a cup with the boiling water and leave to stand while you make the custard.

2 Whisk the egg yolks, sugar and cornflour with a little of the milk in a bowl. Pour the milk into a pan, bring almost to the boil, then pour over the yolk mixture, stirring. Return the mixture to the pan and cook over a very gentle heat, stirring until the custard thickens. Do not let it boil or it may curdle.

3 Stir in the saffron, with its liquid, then cover the surface of the custard with greaseproof (waxed) paper and leave it to cool. Chill until it is very cold.

4 BY HAND: Whip the cream and fold into the custard. Add the apricots and nuts and pour the mixture into a container. Freeze for 3–4 hours, beating twice as it thickens and return to the freezer.

USING AN ICE CREAM MAKER: Stir in the cream and churn until thick. Add the apricots and nuts and churn for 5 minutes more until well mixed. Spoon into a plastic tub or similar freezerproof container and freeze overnight.

5 Transfer to the refrigerator 30 minutes before serving, to soften. Scoop into glasses and serve with amaretti, if using.

COOK'S TIP *This ice cream looks most attractive served in small glasses or little glass cups with handles.*

Ginger and Kiwi Water Ice

Freshly grated root ginger gives a lively, aromatic flavour to water ices and ice creams. Here, it is combined with kiwi fruit to make a refreshing dessert.

SERVES SIX

INGREDIENTS

150g | 2oz FRESH ROOT GINGER

115g | 4oz | ½ cup CASTER (SUPERFINE) SUGAR

300ml | ½ pint | 1¼ cups WATER

5 KIWI FRUIT

MINT SPRIGS or CHOPPED KIWI FRUIT, to decorate

1 Peel the ginger and grate it finely. Put the sugar and water in a pan and heat gently until the sugar has dissolved. Add the ginger and cook for 1 minute, then cool. Strain into a bowl and chill.

2 Peel the kiwi fruit and blend until smooth. Add the purée to the chilled syrup and mix well.

3 BY HAND: Pour the mixture into a container and freeze for 3–4 hours, beating twice as it thickens. Return to the freezer until ready to serve.

USING AN ICE CREAM MAKER: Churn the mixture until it thickens. Transfer to a plastic tub or similar freezerproof container and freeze until ready to serve.

4 Spoon into glasses, decorate with mint sprigs or chopped kiwi fruit, and serve.

Chilli Water Ice

Served during or after dinner, this unusual but refreshing water ice will become a talking point.

SERVES SIX

INGREDIENTS

1 FRESH RED CHILLI

finely grated rind and juice of 2 LEMONS

finely grated rind and juice of 2 LIMES

225g | 8oz | 1 cup CASTER (SUPERFINE) SUGAR

750ml | 1¼ pints | 3 cups WATER

PARED LEMON or LIME RIND, to decorate

1 Cut the chilli in half, removing all the seeds and any pith with a small sharp knife, and then chop the flesh very finely.

2 Put the chilli, lemon and lime rind, sugar and water in a heavy pan. Heat gently and stir while the sugar dissolves. Bring to the boil, then simmer for 2 minutes without stirring. Leave to cool.

3 Add lemon and lime juice to the chilli syrup and chill until very cold.

4 BY HAND: Pour the mixture into a container and freeze for 3–4 hours, beating twice as it thickens. Return to the freezer until ready to serve.

USING AN ICE CREAM MAKER: Churn the mixture until it holds its shape. Scrape into a container and freeze until ready to serve.

5 To serve, spoon into glasses; decorate with the citrus rind.

COOK'S TIP *Use a medium-hot chilli rather than any of the fiery varieties. For an added kick, drizzle with tequila or vodka before serving. To avoid getting chilli juice on your skin wash your hands after dealing with them.*

Turkish Delight Water Ice

Anyone who likes Turkish delight will adore the taste and aroma of this intriguing dessert. Because of its sweetness, it is best served in small portions and is delicious with after-dinner coffee.

5 Spoon the water ice into the cups and tap them lightly on the surface to compact the mixture. Cover with the overlapping film and freeze for at least 3 hours or overnight.

6 Make a paper piping (icing) bag. Put the white chocolate in a heatproof bowl and melt it over a pan of gently simmering water.

7 Meanwhile, remove the ices from the freezer, let them stand at room temperature for 5 minutes, then pull them out of the cups. Transfer to serving plates and peel away the clear film. Spoon the melted chocolate into the piping bag, snip off the tip and scribble a design on the water ice and the plate. Scatter the sugared almonds over and serve.

SERVES EIGHT

INGREDIENTS

250g | 9oz ROSE-WATER-FLAVOURED TURKISH DELIGHT

25g | 1oz | 2 tbsp CASTER (SUPERFINE) SUGAR

750ml | 1¼ pints | 3 cups WATER

30ml | 2 tbsp LEMON JUICE

50g | 2oz WHITE CHOCOLATE, broken into pieces

roughly chopped SUGARED ALMONDS, to decorate

1 Cut the cubes of Turkish delight into small pieces. Put half the pieces in a heavy pan with the sugar. Pour in half the water. Heat gently until the Turkish delight has completely dissolved.

2 Cool, then stir in the lemon juice with the remaining water and Turkish delight. Chill well.

3 BY HAND: Pour the mixture into a container and freeze for 3–4 hours, beating twice as it thickens. Return to the freezer until ready to serve.

USING AN ICE CREAM MAKER: Churn the mixture until it holds its shape. Scrape into a container and freeze until ready to serve.

4 Meanwhile, dampen eight small plastic cups or glasses, then line them with clear film (plastic wrap).

COOK'S TIP *You will probably find it easiest to use scissors to cut the cubes of Turkish delight into smaller pieces, rather than a knife.*

Mulled Wine Ice

This dramatic-looking dessert provides a brief and welcome respite from the general overindulgence that takes place during the festive season, or any other celebration. It is spicy and flavoursome, with quite a powerful kick to revive you from any seasonal sluggishness!

SERVES SIX

INGREDIENTS

1 bottle MEDIUM RED WINE

2 CLEMENTINES or
1 LARGE ORANGE

16 WHOLE CLOVES

2 CINNAMON STICKS, HALVED

1 APPLE, roughly chopped

5ml | 1 tsp MIXED (APPLE PIE)
SPICE

75g | 3oz | scant ½ cup
LIGHT MUSCOVADO
(BROWN) SUGAR

150ml | ¼ pint | ⅔ cup WATER

200ml | 7fl oz | scant 1 cup
FRESHLY SQUEEZED
ORANGE JUICE

45ml | 3 tbsp BRANDY

1 Pour the bottle of wine into a pan. Stud the clementines or orange with the cloves, then cut in half. Add to the wine, with the cinnamon sticks, apple, spice, sugar and water. Heat gently, stirring occasionally, until all the sugar has dissolved.

2 Cover the pan and cook the mixture gently for 15 minutes. Remove from the heat and leave to cool.

3 Strain the mixture into a large bowl, then stir in the orange juice and brandy. Chill until very cold.

4 BY HAND: Pour the mixture into a container and freeze for 3–4 hours, beating twice as it thickens. Return to the freezer until ready to serve.

USING AN ICE CREAM MAKER: Churn the mixture until it thickens. Transfer to a plastic tub or similar freezerproof container and freeze until ready to serve.

5 To serve, spoon or scoop into small glasses and decorate with strips of pared orange rind.

Rose Geranium Marquise

Rose geranium leaves give this ice cream a delicate, scented flavour. If you can't find savoiardi biscuits, ordinary sponge finger biscuits can be used instead. As they tend to be smaller, you may need to adjust the size of the marquise accordingly.

SERVES EIGHT

INGREDIENTS

225g | 8oz | generous 1 cup
CASTER (SUPERFINE) SUGAR

400ml | 14fl oz | 1¾ cups WATER

24 FRESH ROSE
GERANIUM LEAVES

45ml | 3 tbsp LEMON JUICE

250g | 9oz | generous 1 cup
MASCARPONE CHEESE

300ml | ½ pint | 1¼ cups
DOUBLE (HEAVY) or
WHIPPING CREAM

200g | 7oz SAVOIARDI or
SPONGE (LADY)
FINGER BISCUITS

90g | 3½oz | scant 1 cup
ALMONDS, finely chopped
and toasted

GERANIUM FLOWERS
and ICING (CONFECTIONERS')
SUGAR, to decorate

1 Put the sugar and water in a heavy pan and heat gently, stirring occasionally, until the sugar has dissolved. Add the geranium leaves and cook gently for 2 minutes. Leave to cool.

2 Strain the geranium syrup into a measuring jug and add the lemon juice. Put the mascarpone in a bowl and beat it until softened. Gradually beat in 150ml | ¼ pint | ⅔ cup of the syrup mixture. Whip the cream until it forms peaks, then fold it into the mascarpone mixture. At this stage the mixture should hold its shape. If necessary, whip the mixture a little more.

3 Spoon a little of the mixture on to a flat, freezerproof serving plate and spread it out to form a 21 x 12cm | 8½ x 4½in rectangle. Pour the remaining syrup into a shallow bowl. Arrange a third of the biscuits over the rectangle, having first dipped them in the syrup until they are very moist but not actually disintegrating.

4 Spread another thin layer of the cream mixture over the biscuits. Set aside 15ml | 1 tbsp of the nuts for the topping. Scatter half the remainder over the cream. Make a further two layers of syrup-steeped biscuits, sandwiching them with more cream and the remaining nuts, but leaving enough cream mixture to coat the dessert completely.

5 Spread the remaining cream mixture over the top and sides of the cake until it is evenly coated. Sprinkle with the reserved nuts. Freeze the marquise for at least 4 hours or overnight.

6 Transfer the marquise to the refrigerator for 30 minutes before serving, so that it softens slightly. Scatter with geranium flowers, dust with icing sugar, and serve in slices.

COOK'S TIP *Lemon geranium leaves can also be used for this recipe, but other varieties of geranium are not suitable.*

Elderflower and Lime Yogurt Ice

These fragrant flower heads have a wonderful flavour, but they are only in season for a very short time.

Fortunately, good quality bought or home-made elderflower cordial is readily available and combines

beautifully with limes to make a very refreshing iced dessert.

SERVES SIX

INGREDIENTS

4 EGG YOLKS

50g | 2oz | ¼ cup CASTER (SUPERFINE) SUGAR

10ml | 2 tsp CORNFLOUR (CORSTARCH)

300ml | ½ pint | 1¼ cups MILK

finely grated rind and juice of 2 LIMES, plus extra rind to decorate

150ml | ¼ pint | ⅔ cup ELDERFLOWER CORDIAL

200ml | 7fl oz | scant 1 cup GREEK (US PLAIN) YOGURT

150ml | ¼ pint | ⅔ cup DOUBLE (HEAVY) CREAM

2 Pour the custard into a bowl and add the lime rind and juice. Pour in the elderflower cordial and mix lightly. Cover the surface of the mixture with greaseproof (waxed) paper. Leave to cool, then chill until very cold.

3 BY HAND: Whip the yogurt and cream and fold into the custard Pour the mixture into a container and freeze for 3–4 hours, beating twice as it thickens. Scoop into individual dishes and return to the freezer until ready to serve.

USING AN ICE CREAM MAKER: Stir the yogurt and cream into the chilled mixture and churn until it thickens. Transfer to individual dishes and freeze until required.

4 Transfer the yogurt ice to the refrigerator 30 minutes before serving. Decorate with the grated lime rind and serve.

COOK'S TIP *Yogurt gives this ice a slightly tangier flavour than cream, but use all cream if you prefer.*

1 Whisk the egg yolks in a bowl with the sugar, cornflour and a little of the milk. Pour the remaining milk into a heavy pan, bring it to the boil, then pour it over the yolk mixture, whisking constantly. Return the mixture to the pan and cook over a very gentle heat, stirring constantly until the custard thickens. Do not let it boil or it may curdle.

Pomegranate and
Orange Flower Water Creams

Take advantage of the availability of fresh pomegranates when in season to make this wonderfully coloured dessert. The colour will range from pastel pink to vibrant cerise, depending on the type of pomegranates used but whatever shade you achieve the finished result will be very impressive.

SERVES SIX

INGREDIENTS

10ml | 2 tsp CORNFLOUR
(CORNSTARCH)

300ml | ½ pint | 1¼ cups MILK

25g | 1oz | 2 tbsp CASTER
(SUPERFINE) SUGAR

2 LARGE POMEGRANATES

30ml | 2 tbsp ORANGE
FLOWER WATER

75ml | 5 tbsp GRENADINE

300ml | ½ pint | 1¼ cups
WHIPPING CREAM

extra POMEGRANATE SEEDS and
ORANGE FLOWER WATER,
to serve

1 Put the cornflour in a pan and blend to a paste with a little of the milk. Stir in the remaining milk and the sugar and cook, stirring constantly until thickened. Pour into a bowl, cover the surface with greaseproof (waxed) paper and leave to cool.

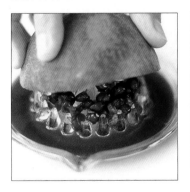

2 Cut the pomegranates in half and squeeze out the juice, using a lemon squeezer. Add the juice to the cornflour mixture, with the orange flower water, grenadine and cream. Stir lightly to mix.

3 BY HAND: Stir to mix; pour into a container. Freeze for 3–4 hours, beating twice as it thickens.

USING AN ICE CREAM MAKER: Churn the mixture until it is thick enough to hold its shape.

4 Spoon the ice cream into one large, or six individual freezerproof serving dishes and freeze for at least 2 hours, or overnight.

5 Transfer the creams to the refrigerator 30 minutes before serving, to allow them to soften. Top each with pomegranate seeds tossed in the extra orange flower water.

VARIATION *To accentuate the Middle-Eastern flavour of this dessert, the seeds from 12 cardamom pods can be added with the orange flower water.*

iced drinks

Keep a supply of classic ice creams
and sorbets for making a whole
range of exciting drinks. Blend with
a splash of liqueur for a cooler
drink with a kick, scoop into
glasses and top up with fizz,
or mix with fruit for a
wonderful drink and
dessert in one.

Iced Margaritas

This smooth, cooling drink has all the punch of Mexico's renowned cocktail! Serve it in tall, slim glasses with a capacity of about 200ml/7fl oz/scant 1 cup.

SERVES TWO

INGREDIENTS

35ml | 7 tsp FRESHLY SQUEEZED
LIME JUICE

CASTER (SUPERFINE) SUGAR,
for frosting

4 LIME and 4 LEMON SLICES

60ml | 4 tbsp TEQUILA

30ml | 2 tbsp COINTREAU

6–8 small scoops of ORANGE or
LIME SORBET (SHERBET)

150ml | ¼ pint | ⅔ cup CHILLED
LEMONADE

sprigs of LEMON BALM,
to decorate

1 Brush the rims of two tall glasses with 5ml | 1 tsp of the lime juice. Spread out the sugar on a plate. Dip the rims of the glasses in the sugar to give a frosted edge.

2 Carefully add two lime and two lemon slices to each glass, standing them on end, so they will be fully visible through the glass.

3 Mix the tequila, Cointreau and remaining lime juice in a bowl. Scoop the sorbet into the glasses.

4 Spoon an equal quantity of the tequila mixture into each glass. Top up with the lemonade and serve immediately, decorated with lemon balm.

VARIATION *For a "shorter" version of this drink, use cocktail glasses and just one scoop of sorbet. The rims of the glasses can be frosted with salt instead of sugar, as for traditional Margaritas.*

Gin and Lemon Fizz

If gin and tonic is your tipple, try this chilled alternative. The fruit and flower ice cubes make a lively decoration for any iced drink.

SERVES TWO

INGREDIENTS

mixture of small EDIBLE
BERRIES or CURRANTS

pieces of thinly pared
LEMON or ORANGE RIND

tiny edible FLOWERS

4 scoops of LEMON SORBET
(SHERBET)

30ml | 2 tbsp GIN

about 120ml | 4fl oz | ½ cup
CHILLED TONIC WATER

1 To make the decorated ice cubes, place each fruit, piece of rind or flower in a section of an ice cube tray. Carefully fill with water and freeze for several hours until the cubes are solid.

2 Divide the sorbet between two cocktail glasses or use small tumblers, with a capacity of about 150ml | ¼ pint | ⅔ cup.

3 Spoon over the gin and add a couple of the ornamental ice cubes to each glass. Top up with tonic water and serve immediately.

COOK'S TIP *When making the ice cubes, choose small herb flowers such as borage or mint, or edible flowers such as rose geraniums, primulas or rose buds.*

Lemonade on Ice

Home-made lemonade may not be fizzy, but it has a fresh, tangy flavour, unmatched by bought drinks.

The basic lemonade will keep well in the refrigerator for up to two weeks and makes a

thirst-quenching drink at any time of day.

SERVES SIX

INGREDIENTS

6 LEMONS

225g | 8oz | 1 cup CASTER
(SUPERFINE) SUGAR

1.75 litres | 3 pints | 7½ cups
BOILING WATER

For each iced drink

4 scoops of LEMON SORBET
(SHERBET)

THIN LEMON and LIME SLICES

3 ICE CUBES, crushed

MINT SPRIGS, to decorate

VARIATION *Use freshly squeezed lime juice instead of lemon juice or bruise some mint leaves and add them to the syrup for a subtle mint flavour. For pink lemonade add a few drops of grenadine to each glass when serving.*

1 Start by making the lemonade. Wash the lemons and dry them thoroughly. Pare all the lemons thinly, avoiding the bitter white pith, and put the rind in a large heatproof bowl. Add the sugar. Squeeze the lemons and set the juice aside.

2 Pour the measured boiling water over the lemon rinds and sugar. Stir until the sugar dissolves. Leave to cool, then stir in the lemon juice. Strain the lemonade into a large jug and chill.

3 For each serving of iced lemonade, place four scoops of sorbet in a tall glass and tuck some lemon and lime slices down the sides. Add the crushed ice. Top up each glass with about 200ml | 7fl oz | scant 1 cup of the lemonade. Decorate with mint sprigs and a few extra halved lemon and lime slices.

Cranberry, Cinnamon and Ginger Spritzer

Partially freezing fruit juice gives it a wonderfully slushy texture that is very refreshing. The combination of cranberry and apple juice contributes a tart, clean flavour that's not too sweet.

SERVES FOUR

INGREDIENTS

600ml | 1 pint | 2½ cups
CHILLED CRANBERRY JUICE

150ml | ¼ pint | ⅔ cup
CLEAR APPLE JUICE

4 CINNAMON STICKS

about 400ml | 14fl oz | 1⅔ cups
CHILLED GINGER ALE

a few FRESH or FROZEN
CRANBERRIES,
to decorate

1 Pour the cranberry juice into a shallow freezerproof container and freeze for about 2 hours or until a thick layer of ice crystals has formed around the edges.

2 Mash with a fork to break up the ice, then return the mixture to the freezer for a further 2–3 hours until almost solid.

3 Pour the apple juice into a small pan, add 2 cinnamon sticks and bring to just below boiling point. Pour into a jug and leave to cool, then remove the cinnamon sticks and set them aside with the other cinnamon sticks. Chill the juice until very cold.

4 Spoon the cranberry ice into a food processor. Add the apple juice and blend very briefly until slushy.

5 Pile into cocktail glasses or flutes, top up with chilled ginger ale and decorate with the fresh or frozen cranberries. Pop a long cinnamon stick into each glass, to use as a swizzle stick.

VARIATION *As an alternative decoration, thread cranberries on four cocktail sticks (toothpicks) and add one to each glass instead of a cinnamon stick.*

Soft Fruit and Ginger Cup

*A colourful medley of soft fruits steeped in vodka and
served with orange water ice and ginger ale.*

SERVES FOUR

INGREDIENTS

115g | 4oz | 1 cup
STRAWBERRIES, hulled

115g | 4oz | ⅔ cup
RASPBERRIES, hulled

50g | 2oz | ½ cup BLUEBERRIES

15ml | 1 tbsp CASTER
(SUPERFINE) SUGAR

90ml | 6 tbsp VODKA

600ml | 1 pint | 2½ cups GINGER ALE

4 large scoops of ORANGE SORBET
(SHERBET)

about 8 ICE CUBES

20ml | 4 tsp GRENADINE

4 PHYSALIS FLOWERS, to decorate

1 Cut the strawberries in half and
put them in a bowl with the
raspberries, blueberries and sugar.
Pour over the vodka and toss
lightly. Cover and chill for at least
30 minutes.

2 Put the ginger ale and sorbet in
a blender or food processor and
process until smooth. Pour into
four bowl-shaped glasses and add a
couple of ice cubes to each glass
of sorbet mixture.

3 Spoon a teaspoon of grenadine
over the ice cubes in each glass,
then spoon the vodka-steeped
fruits on top of the sorbet mixture
and ice cubes. Decorate each glass
with a physalis and serve the
drinks immediately.

VARIATION *Any combination of soft
fruit can be used for this iced drink.
Blackberries, for example, would also
work very well.*

Sparkling Peach Melba

*This refreshing fruit fizz is an excellent choice for summer celebrations.
As with most soft fruit recipes, its success depends on using the ripest,
tastiest peaches and raspberries available.*

SERVES FOUR

INGREDIENTS

3 RIPE PEACHES

90ml | 6 tbsp ORANGE JUICE

75g | 3oz | ½ cup RASPBERRIES

10ml | 2 tsp ICING
(CONFECTIONERS') SUGAR

about 500ml | 17fl oz |
2¼ cups RASPBERRY SORBET
(SHERBET)

about 400ml | 14fl oz | 1⅓ cups
MEDIUM SPARKLING
CHILLED WHITE WINE

FRESH MINT SPRIGS,
to decorate

1 Put the peaches in a heatproof
bowl and pour over boiling water
to cover. Leave for 60 seconds,
then drain the peaches and peel off
the skins.

2 Cut the fruit in half and remove
the stones. Chop the peach halves
roughly and purée them with the
orange juice in a food processor or
blender until smooth. Scrape the
purée into a bowl.

3 Put the raspberries in the food
processor or blender. Add the icing
sugar and process until smooth.
Press the raspberry purée through
a sieve into a bowl. Chill both
purées for at least 1 hour.

4 Spoon the chilled peach purée
into four tall glasses.

5 Add scoops of sorbet to come to
the top of the glasses. Spoon the
raspberry purée around the sorbet.

6 Top up each glass with sparkling
wine. Decorate with the mint
sprigs and serve.

VARIATION *When fresh ripe peaches
are unavailable, use canned peach
halves in juice or light syrup.*

Iced Mango Lassi

Based on a traditional Indian drink, this is excellent with spicy food, or as a welcome cooler at any time of day.

The yogurt ice that forms the basis of this drink is a useful recipe to add to your repertoire –

it is lighter and fresher than cream-based ices.

SERVES THREE TO FOUR

INGREDIENTS

For the yogurt ice

175g | 6oz | ¾ cup CASTER
(SUPERFINE) SUGAR

150ml | ¼ pint | ⅔ cup WATER

2 LEMONS

500ml | 17fl oz | generous 2 cups
GREEK (US STRAINED PLAIN)
YOGURT

For each drink

120ml | 4fl oz | ½ cup MANGO JUICE

2–3 ICE CUBES
(optional)

FRESH MINT SPRIGS and
WEDGES of MANGO, to serve

1 To make the yogurt ice, put the sugar and water in a pan and heat gently, stirring occasionally, until the sugar has dissolved. Pour the syrup into a jug. Leave to cool, then chill until very cold.

2 Grate the lemons and then squeeze them. Add the rind and juice to the chilled syrup and stir well to mix.

3 BY HAND: Pour the syrup mixture into a container and freeze until thickened. Beat in the yogurt and return to the freezer until thick enough to scoop.

USING AN ICE CREAM MAKER: Churn the mixture until it thickens. Stir in the yogurt and churn for 2 minutes more until well mixed. Transfer to a plastic tub or similar freezerproof container and freeze.

4 To make each lassi, briefly blend the mango juice with three small scoops of the yogurt ice in a food processor or blender until just smooth. Pour the mixture into a tall glass or tumbler and add the ice cubes, if using.

5 Top each drink with another scoop of the yogurt ice and decorate. Serve at once.

VARIATION *Add one small chopped banana when blending the ingredients together for a delicious and substantial summer smoothie.*

COOK'S TIP *Make sure you buy Greek yogurt for this drink as it adds a lovely, sharp tang.*

Tropical Fruit Sodas

For many children, scoops of vanilla ice cream, served
in a froth of lemonade would make the perfect treat.
This more elaborate version will appeal to adults too.

SERVES FOUR

INGREDIENTS

10ml | 2 tsp GRANULATED SUGAR

1 PAPAYA

1 SMALL RIPE MANGO

2 PASSION FRUIT

8 large scoops of
VANILLA ICE CREAM

8 large scoops of CARAMEL or
TOFFEE ICE CREAM

about 400ml | 14fl oz | 1⅔ cups
CHILLED LEMONADE or
SODA WATER

1 Line a baking sheet with foil.
Make four small mounds of sugar
on the foil, using about 2.5ml |
½ tsp each time and spacing them
well apart. Place under a moderate
grill (broiler) for about 2 minutes
until the sugar mounds have
turned to a pale golden caramel.

2 Immediately swirl each pool of
caramel with just the tip of a
cocktail stick (toothpick) or skewer
to give a slightly feathery finish.
Leave to cool.

3 Cut the papaya in half. Scoop
out and discard the seeds, then
remove the skin and chop the flesh.
Skin the mango, cut the flesh off
the stone and chop into bite-size
chunks. Mix the papaya and mango
in a bowl.

4 Cut each passion fruit in half
and scoop the pulp into the bowl
of fruit. Mix well, cover and chill
until ready to serve.

5 Divide the chilled fruit mixture
among four large tumblers, each
with a capacity of about 300ml |
½ pint | 1¼ cups.

6 Add one scoop of each type of
ice cream to each glass. Peel the
caramel decorations carefully away
from the foil and press gently into
the ice cream. Top up with
lemonade or soda and serve.

VARIATIONS *Use a mixture of*
strawberries and raspberries or other
more familiar fruits for children. For
adults, a splash of vodka or kirsch can
be added to the fruits.

Snowball

For many of us, a "snowball" is a drink we indulge in once or twice at Christmas time. This iced version,

enhanced with melting vanilla ice cream, lime and nutmeg, may provide the motivation

for drinking advocaat on other occasions too.

SERVES FOUR

INGREDIENTS

8 scoops of
VANILLA ICE CREAM

120ml | 4fl oz | ½ cup ADVOCAAT

60ml | 4 tbsp FRESHLY SQUEEZED
LIME JUICE

FRESHLY GRATED NUTMEG

about 300ml | ½ pint | 1¼ cups
CHILLED LEMONADE

1 Put half the vanilla ice cream in a food processor or blender and add the advocaat and the lime juice, with plenty of freshly grated nutmeg. Process the mixture briefly until well combined.

2 Scoop the remaining ice cream into four medium tumblers. Spoon over the advocaat mixture and top up the glasses with lemonade. Sprinkle with more nutmeg and serve immediately.

COOK'S TIP *Freshly grated nutmeg has a warm, nutty aroma and flavour that works as well in creamy drinks as it does in sweet and savoury dishes. A small nutmeg grater is a worthwhile investment if you don't have one.*

Strawberry Daiquiri

Based on the classic cocktail, this version is a wonderful drink which retains the essential ingredients

of rum and lime and combines them with fresh strawberries and strawberry ice cream

to create a thick iced fruit purée.

SERVES FOUR

INGREDIENTS

225g | 8oz | 2 cups
STRAWBERRIES, hulled

5ml | 1 tsp CASTER
(SUPERFINE) SUGAR

120ml | 4fl oz | ½ cup
BACARDI RUM

30ml | 2 tbsp FRESHLY
SQUEEZED LIME JUICE

8 scoops of STRAWBERRY
ICE CREAM

about 150ml | ¼ pint | ⅔ cup
CHILLED LEMONADE

extra STRAWBERRIES
and LIME SLICES,
to decorate

1 Blend the strawberries with the sugar in a food processor or blender, then press the purée through a sieve into a bowl. Return the strawberry purée to the blender with the rum, lime juice and half the strawberry ice cream. Blend until smooth.

2 Scoop the remaining strawberry ice cream into four cocktail glasses or small tumblers and pour over the blended mixture.

3 Top up with lemonade, decorate with fresh strawberries and lime slices, and serve.

VARIATION *Orange-flavoured liqueur or vodka could be used instead of the rum, if you prefer.*

COOKS TIP *For the best results use luxury ice cream, or preferably, homemade. This will avoid the risk of a synthetic flavour and garish colour.*

Index

a

Advocaat 124
Alaskas 54
almond biscuits 54
almond essence 24, 29, 55, 74,
    82, 85, 96
almonds 45, 64, 79, 82, 96, 105,
    108, 110
amaretti biscuits 38, 74, 105
amaretto liqueur 96
Apple Ice Cream with
    Cinnamon Bread 61
apple juice 70, 119
apples 50, 61
apricots 38, 42–43,
    54, 105
Armagnac 33

b

Baby Alaskas with Liqueured
    Apricots 54
Bacardi rum 124
Baked Bananas with Ice
    Cream 56
baking powder 44, 55,
    64, 82
bananas 56, 122
Basil and Orange
    Granita 102
basil leaves 102
baskets 16–17
bay leaves 41
biscuits 18, 101

blackberries 60, 120
Blackcurrant and Meringue
    Trifles 80
blackcurrant sorbet
    as ingredient 80, 89
blackcurrants 92
blueberries 64, 68, 120
Blueberry and Vanilla
    Crumble Torte 64
bombes, recipes 26–7, 30
borage 94, 116
Brandied Apple Charlotte 50
brazil nuts 41
bread 61
breadcrumbs 41
brioche buns 62
brownies 42

c

Caramel and Pecan
    Terrine 28
cardamom 34, 104, 113
Cassata 24
cherries 41, 42, 74
    black 62
    glacé 24, 45
chestnut purée 26
Chilli Sorbet 106
chillis 106
chocolate
    drinking chocolate 62, 78
    milk chocolate 72
    plain chocolate 26, 33, 39,
        45, 47, 51, 56, 72, 74, 79

    white chocolate 42, 68, 108
Chocolate and Brandied
    Fig Torte 39
Chocolate Ice Cream in
    Florentine Baskets 79
Chocolate Millefeuille
    Slice 75
Chocolate, Rum and Raisin
    Roulade 51
chocolate sponge cake 47
Chocolate Teardrops with
    Cherry Sauce 74
cigarettes russes 18
cinnamon 30, 61, 62, 80, 93,
    109, 119
citrus fruit 24
    see also clementines, lemons,
        kumquats, limes, oranges,
        grapefuit
Classic Coffee Ice Cream
    as ingredient 72
Classic Dark Chocolate Ice
    Cream
    as ingredient 62, 68, 72, 79
Classic Vanilla Ice Cream
    as ingredient 48, 54, 56–8,
        60, 62, 64, 72, 76, 82, 84,
        123, 124
clementines 80, 95, 109
cloves 30, 109
cocoa 33, 39, 42, 153–545–7,
    51, 68
Coconut and Lemon Grass Ice
    Cream 34
Coconut and Passion Fruit
    Alaska 55
Coconut Ice Cream with
    Mango Sauce 85
coconut milk 34
coconuts 25, 55, 85

d

coffee 33, 78
Cointreau 26, 44, 47, 54, 65, 71,
    90, 92, 105, 116
colouring 24, 40, 70, 118
cones 76
cranberries 41, 71, 119
    cranberry juice 119
Cranberry, Cinnamon and
    Ginger Spritzer 119
Cranberry Sorbet in Lace
    Pancakes 71
cream cheese 32, 40, 61
crème de cassis 89
crème fraîche 39, 75, 100
croissants 56
cucumber 94

d

dates 39
decoration techniques 19–21
Disaronno Amaretto
    liqueur 96
Double White Chocolate Ice
    Cream
    as ingredient 68

e

Elderflower and Lime Yogurt
    Ice 112
elderflower cordial 112
elderflowers 70

f

Fig, Port and Clementine
    Sundaes 80
figs 39, 80

Filo, Ice Cream and
    Mincemeat Parcels 58
filo pastry 58
flowers 69
    see also borage, elderflower,
        geranium, lavender,
        lemon geranium, marigold,
        nasturtium, primrose,
        primula, rose, rosemary,
        violet
freezing 9
fromage frais 42
fruit 13, 14
    glacé 24, 45, 79
    see also apples, bananas,
        blackberries, blackcurrants,
        blueberries, citrus fruits,
        cranberries, dates, figs,
        gooseberries, grenadines,
        kiwi fruit, mangoes,
        melon, passion fruit,
        pawpaw, peach, pear,
        physalis, pomegranates,
        prunes, raspberries,
        redcurrants, rhubarb,
        strawberries,
        whitecurrants

g

gâteaux recipes 44–9
gelatine 88, 90
geranium flowers 110
gin 74, 116
ginger, glacé 79
ginger ale 119, 120
Ginger and Kiwi
    Sorbet 106
ginger biscuits 54
ginger wine 40
gingerbread 84
gingersnap biscuits 39
golden syrup 47, 56, 79
gooseberries 70
Gooseberry and Elderflower
    Sorbet 70
granitas
    how to make 15
    recipes 96, 102
grapefruit 102
grenadine 113, 118, 120

h

Hazelnut Cones with Vanilla
    Ice Cream and Hazelnut
    Caramel Sauce 18876
hazelnuts 56, 72, 76
herb flowers 69

herbs 100
honey ice cream 54
hot ice cream puddings
    recipes 52–65

i

Ice Cream Croissants with
    Chocolate Sauce 56
ice cream makers 8–9
Ice Cream with Hot Cherry
    Sauce 62
ice creams, how to make 12
ice cubes 69
Iced Christmas Torte 41
Iced Clementines 95
Iced Coconut Mousse 25
Iced Coffee Cups 78
iced drinks 114–125
Iced Mango Lassi 122
Iced Margaritas 116
Iced Melon with
    Pimm's 94
Iced Raspberry and Almond
    Trifle 82
Iced Strawberry and Lemon
    Curd Gâteau 44
Iced Summer Pudding 89
Iced Vanilla Brûlées 72
India 122

k

Kahlúa 33, 78
kirsch 123
kiwi fruit 106
Kulfi 34
kumquats 29

l

lavender 101
Lavender and Honey Ice
    Cream 101
Layered Chocolate and
    Chestnut Bombes 26
layering 26
Lemon and Cardamom Ice
    Cream 104
lemon balm 40, 95, 97, 104, 116
lemon curd 44
lemon geranium leaves 110
lemon grass 34
lemon juice 106
lemon rind 106, 116
Lemon Sorbet
    as ingredient 92, 116, 118
Lemon Sorbet Cups with
    Summer Fruits 92
lemonade 116, 123, 124

Lemonade on Ice 118
lemons 58, 61, 62, 95, 104, 116,
    118, 122
lime juice 34, 106, 116,
    118, 124
lime rind 106
lime sorbet 116
limes 34, 112, 118, 124
liqueurs 44, 47, 54, 78, 90, 92,
    96, 105

m

Madeira 38
Madeira cake 50, 89
mango juice 122
mangoes 55, 85, 122, 123
Maple and Walnut Meringue
    Gâteau 48
maple syrup 48, 75
marigolds 69
marzipan 29
Marzipan and Kumquat
    Terrine 29
mascarpone cheese 26, 65,
    82, 110
melons 94
meringues 25, 48, 80
    meringue nests 48

milk
    coconut milk 34
    full cream milk 29, 34, 72
mincemeat 58
Miniature Choc-ices 72
mint 40, 61, 80, 95, 97, 106, 116,
    118, 120, 122
Mocha, Prune and Armagnac
    Terrine 33
mousses 25, 88, 90
Mulled Wine Sorbet 109

n

nasturtiums 69
nectarines 32
nougat 42
nutmeg 124
nuts
    see also almonds, brazil nuts,
        chestnuts, coconuts,
        hazelnuts, pecan nuts,
        walnuts

o

oil 58, 65, 71
Orange Crêpes with
    Mascarpone Cream 65

orange flower water 30, 113
orange juice 25, 47, 65, 71, 82, 85, 95, 102, 109, 120
orange liqueurs 47, 54, 71, 90, 92, 105
orange rind 47, 109, 116
orange sorbet 65, 80, 116, 120
oranges 30, 62, 65, 90, 102, 109

p

pancakes 71
pansies 69
passion fruit 25, 55, 88, 123
Passion Fruit Mousses 88
pastry 58
pawpaws 123
Peach and Almond Granitas 96
Peach, Blackberry and Ice Cream Gratin 60
Peach Mousse Cakes 90
peaches 60, 90, 96, 120
Pear and Gingerbread Sundaes 84
pears 58, 84, 93
pecan nuts 28, 75
peel, candied 24
physalis 120
Pimm's No 1 94
Pistachio and Nougat Torte 42
pistachio nuts 42
Pomegranate and Orange Flower Water Creams 113
pomegranates 133
port 41, 80
primroses 69
primulas 69
prunes 33, 39, 41
puff pastry 58
pumpkin purée 30
purées
    see also chestnut purée, pumpkin purée

r

raisins 79, 84
raspberries 42, 47, 48, 82, 92, 120, 123
Raspberry Ice Cream as ingredient 82, 89
Raspberry Mousse Gâteau 46
raspberry sorbet 82, 120
ratafia biscuits 100
redcurrant sorbet 89

redcurrants 48
rhubarb 40
Rhubarb and Ginger Wine Torte 40
rice 72
Rich Chocolate Mousse Gâteau 47
ricotta cheese 45, 50, 97
Rippled Nectarine and Muscovado Terrine 32
rose buds 116
Rose Geranium Marquise 110
rose geraniums 110, 116
rose petals 69
rosemary 100
Rosemary Ice Cream 100
rosewater 34, 42, 108
rum 51, 124
Rum and Raisin Ice Cream as ingredient 51

s

Saffron, Apricot and Almond Cream 105
Savoiardi biscuits 110
sherry 38, 82
Snowball 124
soda water 123
Soft Fruit and Crushed Meringue Gâteau 48
Soft Fruit and Ginger Cup 120
sorbets 69–71
    as ingredient 80, 82, 89, 92, 94
    Cranberry Sorbet in Lace Pancakes 71
    Ginger and Kiwi Sorbet 106
    Gooseberry and Elderflower Sorbet 70
    how to make 14
    Mulled Wine Sorbet 109
    Sorbet in an Ice Bowl 69
    Spiced Sorbet Pears 93
    Turkish Delight Sorbet 108
Sparkling Peach Melba 120
Spiced Sorbet Pears 93
Spicy Pumpkin and Orange Bombe 30
sponge finger biscuits 40, 110
star anise 102
Star Anise and Grapefruit Granita 102
Strawberry Daiquiri 124
Strawberry Ice Cream as ingredient 44, 89, 124

strawberry jam 89, 97
Strawberry Semi-freddo 97
sultanas 41, 50, 84
sundaes 80, 84
Syrupy Brioche Slices with Vanilla Ice Cream 62

t

terrine recipes 28, 29, 32, 33
Tia Maria 78
tonic water 116
tortes 38–43
trifle sponges 42
trifles 80–82
Tropical Fruit Sodas 123
turkish delight 108
Turkish Delight Sorbet 108

v

vanilla custard 56
vanilla essence 26, 61, 64, 72, 76, 97
vanilla pods 72
violets 69
vodka 120, 123

w

Walnut and Vanilla Ice Palmiers 58
Walnut Castles 34
walnuts 34, 48
whisky 46
White Chocolate and Brownie Torte 42
White Chocolate Castles 68
whitecurrants 92
wine 93, 109, 120

y

yogurt
    recipes 80, 82, 97, 112, 122

z

Zabaglione Ice Cream Torte 38
Zucotto 45

CHINESE COOKING

Designed by Justine Davies
Food photography by Peter Barry
Recipes styled by Jacqueline Bellefontaine
Edited by Jillian Stewart
Incidental photography by FPG International

CLB 2709
All rights reserved.
This 1993 edition published by Magna Books,
Magna Road, Wigston, Leicester LE18 4ZH.
© 1993 Colour Library Books Ltd., Godalming,
Surrey, England.
Printed and bound in Singapore.
ISBN 1 85422 486 7

CHINESE COOKING

MAGNA BOOKS

INTRODUCTION

Chinese cuisine is one of world's most ancient styles of cooking, yet it has captured modern tastes with its style and simplicity. Western interest in Chinese cuisine came about relatively recently with the first Chinese immigrants who took their enticing recipes to the four corners of the world. The earliest Chinese "restaurants" were simply kitchens established to feed the immigrant population, but as word spread, everyone began to discover the delights of Chinese food.

It is rather misleading, though, to talk about Chinese food as if it had one distinct identity. A country as vast as China encompasses a whole range of geographical, climatic and social conditions that lead to various regional styles of cooking. Southern, or Cantonese, cooking is perhaps the style most widely known in the West. The climate is warm and the meals light; stir-fried dishes of crisp vegetables and subtle sauces are characteristic, and rice is the staple accompaniment. In the north wheat is the major crop, therefore noodles are eaten more than rice. The region can be very cold, and rich sauces and meat dishes, as well as dumplings and pancakes, add much needed warmth.

The cuisine of western China is presently enjoying great popularity. Szechuan is a mountainous region famous for its peppercorns and chillies, and its cuisine utilises these ingredients to create dishes that are pungent and highly spiced. By contrast, eastern China is blessed with a plentiful and varied harvest, which it uses to create dishes that combine the simplicity of northern cuisine with the creative talents of southern chefs.

There are certain characteristics which are common to all these styles of cooking and form the basis of Chinese cuisine. The use of the stir-frying technique is commonplace. The ingredients are carefully cut up into the appropriate shapes to facilitate quick cooking, then fried in a little oil at a high temperature. The secret of successful stir-frying is good preparation and adding the ingredients in the correct order so that the finished dish retains all the taste, goodness and texture of each ingredient.

Texture is something that is very important to the Chinese, who insist that vegetables retain their 'bite' and they will often add ingredients that have very little taste but add a nice texture. Dried ingredients are important for this purpose, and many of them, such as dried mushrooms, also have a wonderful flavour. Possibly the most popular attribute of Chinese cooking, and one that makes it eminently suitable for everyday meals, is the short cooking time of most recipes. A wok is the best tool for this purpose, but a deep non-stick pan will serve the purpose.

Chinese cooking is popular because it requires so little in the way of expertise and equipment, yet it offers endless variety and taste. So try a taste of Chinese cooking and you will find China's most delicious dishes can easily be prepared without leaving your own kitchen.

Right: the Imperial Palace in Peking is one China's most symbolic buildings. Ordinary Chinese citizens were once banned from even approaching the so-called Forbidden City.

Wonton Soup

Preparation Time: 25-30 minutes **Cooking Time:** 5-10 minutes **Serves:** 6-8

Probably the best-known Chinese soup, this recipe uses pre-made wonton wrappers for ease of preparation.

Ingredients

20-24 wonton wrappers
90g/3oz finely minced chicken
2 tbsps chopped coriander
3 spring onions, finely chopped
1 inch piece fresh ginger,
    peeled and grated

1 egg, lightly beaten
1.5 ltr/2½ pints chicken stock
1 tbsp dark soy sauce
Dash sesame oil
Salt and pepper
Coriander or watercress for garnish

Place all the wonton wrappers on a large, flat surface. Mix together the chicken, chopped coriander, spring onions and ginger. Brush the edges of the wrappers lightly with beaten egg. Place a small mound of mixture on one half of the wrappers and fold the other half over the top to form a triangle. Press with the fingers to seal the edges well.

Bring the stock to the boil in a large saucepan. Add the filled wontons and simmer 5-10 minutes or until they float to the surface. Add remaining ingredients to the soup, using only the leaves of the coriander or watercress for garnish.

The bright lights of the Jumbo floating restaurant in Hong Kong contrasts markedly with the austerity of mainland China's restaurants, only a short distance away.

Barbecued Spare Ribs

Preparation Time: 45 minutes **Cooking Time:** 1 hour **Serves:** 4-6

Although Chinese barbecue sauce is nothing like the tomato-based American-style sauce, these ribs are still tasty cooked on an outdoor grill.

Ingredients

4lbs fresh spare-ribs	2 tbsps dry sherry
45ml/3 tbsps dark soy sauce	¼ tsp five spice powder
90ml/6 tbsps hoisin sauce (Chinese barbecue sauce)	1 tbsp brown sugar
	4-6 spring onions for garnish

First prepare the garnish. Trim the root ends and the dark green tops from the onions. Cut both ends into thin strips, leaving about ½ inch in the middle uncut. Place the onions in ice water for several hours or overnight for the ends to curl up.

Cut the spare-ribs into one-rib pieces. Mix all the remaining ingredients together, pour over the ribs and stir to coat evenly. Allow to stand for 1 hour. Put the spare-rib pieces on a rack in a roasting tin containing 1 pint water and cook in a preheated 180°C/350°F/Gas Mark 4 oven for 30 minutes. Add more hot water to the pan while cooking, if necessary. Turn the ribs over and brush with the remaining sauce. Cook 30 minutes longer, or until tender. Serve garnished with the onion brushes.

Top: China requires a vast amount of food to feed its huge population and for this reason farming still occupies four out of five Chinese workers.

Hot & Sour Soup

Preparation Time: 25 minutes **Cooking Time:** 7-8 minutes **Serves:** 4-6

A very warming soup, this is a favourite in winter in Peking. Add chilli sauce and vinegar to suit your taste.

Ingredients

60g/2oz pork
3 dried Chinese mushrooms, soaked
   in boiling water for 5 minutes
   and chopped
60g/2oz peeled, uncooked prawns
1.5 ltr/2½ pints chicken stock
30g/1oz bamboo shoots, sliced
3 spring onions, shredded
Salt and pepper
1 tbsp sugar

1 tsp dark soy sauce
½ tsp light soy sauce
1-2 tsps chilli sauce
1½ tbsps vinegar
Dash sesame seed oil and
   rice wine or sherry
1 egg, well beaten
2 tbsps water mixed with
   1 tbsp cornflour

Trim any fat from the pork and slice it into shreds about 2-inches long and less than ¼-inch thick. Soak the mushrooms in boiling water until softened. Place the pork in a large pot with the prawns and stock. Bring to the boil and then reduce the heat to allow to simmer gently for 4-5 minutes. Add all the remaining ingredients except for the egg and cornflour and water mixture. Cook a further 1-2 minutes over low heat.

Remove the pan from the heat and add the egg gradually, stirring gently until it forms threads in the soup. Mix a spoonful of the hot soup with the cornstarch and water mixture and add to the soup, stirring constantly. Bring the soup back to simmering point for 1 minute to thicken the cornflour. Serve immediately.

A busy street market in Shanghai. Once little more than a fishing village, it is now one of country's busiest and most overcrowded cities.

Sesame Chicken Wings

Preparation Time: 25 minutes **Cooking Time:** 13-14 minutes **Serves:** 8

This is an economical starter that is also good as a cocktail snack or as a light meal with stir-fried vegetables.

Ingredients
12 chicken wings
1 tbsp salted black beans
1 tbsp water
1 tbsp oil
2 cloves garlic, crushed
2 slices fresh ginger, cut into
    fine shreds

45ml/3 tbsps soy sauce
1½ tbsps dry sherry or rice wine
Large pinch black pepper
1 tbsp sesame seeds

Cut off and discard the wing tips. Cut between the joint to separate into two pieces. Crush the beans and add the water. Leave to stand.

Heat the oil in a wok and add the garlic and ginger. Stir briefly and add the chicken wings. Cook, stirring, until lightly browned, about 3 minutes. Add the soy sauce and wine and cook, stirring, about 30 seconds longer. Add the soaked black beans and pepper. Cover the wok tightly and simmer for about 8-10 minutes. Uncover and turn the heat to high. Continue cooking, stirring until the liquid is almost evaporated and the chicken wings are glazed with sauce. Remove from the heat and sprinkle on sesame seeds. Stir to coat completely and serve. Garnish with spring onions or coriander, if desired.

Top: street markets play a crucial part in Chinese life, with farmers travelling from outlying areas to sell their produce in the towns.

Crab & Sweetcorn Soup

Preparation Time: 10 minutes **Cooking Time:** 8-10 minutes **Serves:** 4-6

Creamy sweetcorn and succulent crabmeat combine to make a velvety rich soup. Whisked egg whites add an interesting texture.

Ingredients

850ml/1½ pints chicken or fish stock
340g/12oz creamed sweetcorn
120g/4oz crabmeat
Salt and pepper
1 tsp light soy sauce

2 tbsps cornflour
3 tbsps water or stock
2 egg whites, whisked
4 spring onions for garnish

Bring the stock to the boil in a large pan. Add the sweetcorn, crabmeat, seasoning and soy sauce. Allow to simmer for 4-5 minutes. Mix the cornflour and water or stock and add a spoonful of the hot soup. Return the mixture to the soup and bring back to the boil. Cook until the soup thickens. Whisk the egg whites until soft peaks form. Stir into the hot soup just before serving. Slice the onions thinly on the diagonal and scatter over the top to serve.

The Chinese are passionate about good food, believing it is one of the roads to long life, and with an emphasis on fresh vegetables, Chinese cooking is certainly healthy.

Spring Rolls

Preparation Time: 50 minutes **Cooking Time:** 20 minutes **Makes:** 12

One of the most popular Chinese hors d'oeuvres, these are delicious dipped in sweet-sour sauce.

Ingredients
Wrappers
120g/4oz strong plain flour
1 egg, beaten

Cold water

Filling
225g/8oz pork, trimmed and finely shredded
120g/4oz prawns, chopped
4 spring onions, finely chopped
2 tsps chopped fresh ginger
120g/4oz Chinese cabbage leaves, shredded

100g/3½oz bean sprouts
1 tbsp light soy sauce
Dash sesame seed oil
1 egg, beaten

To prepare the wrappers, sift the flour into a bowl and make a well in the centre. Add the beaten egg and about 1 tbsp cold water. Begin beating with a wooden spoon, gradually drawing in the flour from the outside to make a smooth dough. Add more water if necessary. Knead the dough until it is elastic and pliable. Place in a covered bowl and chill for about 4 hours or overnight.

When ready to roll out, allow the dough to come back to room temperature. Flour a large work surface well and roll the dough out to about ¼-inch thick. Cut the dough into 12 equal squares and then roll each piece out to a larger square about 6 x 6 inches. The dough should be very thin. Cover while preparing the filling.

Cook the pork in a little of the frying oil for about 2-3 minutes. Add the remaining filling ingredients, except the beaten egg, cook for a further 2-3 minutes and allow to cool. Lay out the wrappers on a clean work surface with one corner of each wrapper facing you. Brush the edges lightly with the beaten egg. Divide the filling among all 12 wrappers, placing it just above the front corner. Fold over the sides like an envelope. Then fold over the point until the filling is completely covered, and roll up as for a Swiss roll. Press all the edges to seal well.

Heat the oil in a deep fat fryer or in a deep pan to 375°F. Depending upon the size of the fryer, place in 2-4 spring rolls and fry until golden brown on both sides. The rolls will float to the surface when one side has browned and should be turned over. Drain thoroughly on paper towels and serve hot.

Pot Sticker Dumplings

Preparation Time: 50 minutes **Cooking Time:** 10-20 minutes **Makes:** 12

So called because they are fried in very little oil, they will stick unless they are brown and crisp on the bottom before they are steamed.

Ingredients
Dumpling Pastry
180g/6oz plain flour
½ tsp salt

3 tbsps oil
Boiling water

Filling
120g/4oz finely ground pork
4 water chestnuts, finely chopped
3 spring onions, finely chopped
½ tsp five spice powder

1 tbsp light soy sauce
1 tsp sugar
1 tsp sesame oil

Sift the flour and salt into a large bowl and make a well in the centre. Pour in the oil and add enough boiling water to make a pliable dough. Add about 4 tbsps water at first and begin stirring with a wooden spoon to gradually incorporate the flour. Add more water as necessary. Knead the dough for about 5 minutes and allow to rest for 30 minutes. Divide the dough into 12 pieces and roll each piece out to a circle about 6 inches in diameter.

Mix all the filling ingredients together and place a mound of filling on half of each circle. Fold over the top and press the edges together firmly. Roll over the joined edges using a twisting motion and press down to seal. Pour about ⅛ inch of oil in a large frying pan, preferably cast iron. When the oil is hot, add the dumplings flat side down and cook until nicely browned. When the underside is brown, add about ⅓ cup water to the pan and cover it tightly. Continue cooking gently for about 5 minutes, or until the top surface of the dumplings is steamed and appears cooked. Serve immediately.

Special Mixed Vegetables

Preparation Time: 25 minutes **Cooking Time:** 2½-3 minutes **Serves:** 4

This dish illustrates the basic stir-frying technique for vegetables. Use other varieties for an equally colourful side dish.

Ingredients

1 tbsp oil
1 clove garlic, crushed
1-inch piece fresh ginger, sliced
4 Chinese cabbage leaves, shredded
60g/2oz flat mushrooms, sliced
60g/2oz bamboo shoots, sliced
3 sticks celery, diagonally sliced
60g/2oz baby corn, cut in half if large

1 small red pepper, cored,
    seeded and thinly sliced
60g/2oz bean sprouts
2 tbsps light soy sauce
Dash sesame oil
Salt and pepper
3 tomatoes, peeled, seeded
    and quartered

Heat the oil in a wok and add the vegetables in the order given, reserving the tomatoes until last. To make it easier to peel the tomatoes, remove the stems and place in boiling water for 5 seconds. Remove from the boiling water with a draining spoon and place in a bowl of cold water. This will make the peels easier to remove. Cut out the core end using a small sharp knife. Cut the tomatoes in half and then in quarters. Use a teaspoon or a serrated edged knife to remove the seeds and the cores. Cook the vegetables for about 2 minutes. Stir in the soy sauce, sesame oil and seasoning and add the tomatoes. Heat through for 30 seconds and serve immediately.

Top: husking corn in Feng Tai village, Shandong province. Life for Chinese farm workers is an endless struggle to make the land as productive as possible.

Fried Rice

Cooking Time: 5-10 minutes   **Serves:** 6-8

A basic recipe for a traditional Chinese accompaniment to stir-fried dishes, this can be made more substantial with the addition of meat, poultry or seafood.

Ingredients

450g/1lb cooked rice, well drained
   and dried
45ml/3 tbsps oil
1 egg, beaten
1 tbsp soy sauce

60g/2oz cooked peas
Salt and pepper
Dash sesame oil
2 spring onions, thinly sliced

Heat a wok and add the oil. Pour in the egg and soy sauce and cook until just beginning to set. Add the rice and peas and stir to coat with the egg mixture. Allow to cook for about 3 minutes, stirring continuously. Add seasoning and sesame oil. Spoon into a serving dish and sprinkle over the spring onions.

The Li River has, over millions of years, carved the limestone rocks into strange and beautiful shapes which rise abruptly from the otherwise flat ground.

Cantonese Egg Fu Yung

Preparation Time: 25 minutes **Cooking Time:** 13 minutes **Serves:** 2-3

As the name suggests, this dish is from Canton. However, fu yung dishes are popular in many other regions of China, too.

Ingredients

5 eggs
60g/2oz shredded cooked meat, poultry or fish
1 stick celery, finely shredded
4 Chinese dried mushrooms, soaked in boiling water for 5 minutes

60g/2oz bean sprouts
1 small onion, thinly sliced
Pinch salt and pepper
1 tsp dry sherry
Oil for frying

Sauce

1 tbsp cornflour dissolved in 3 tbsps cold water
280ml/½ pint chicken stock
1 tsp tomato ketchup

1 tbsp soy sauce
Pinch salt and pepper
Dash sesame oil

Beat the eggs lightly and add the shredded meat and celery. Squeeze all the liquid from the dried mushrooms. Remove the stems and cut the caps into thin slices. Add to the egg mixture along with the bean sprouts and onion. Add a pinch of salt and pepper and the sherry, and stir well.

Heat a wok or frying pan and pour in about 4 tbsps oil. When hot, carefully spoon in about 90ml/3 fl oz of the egg mixture. Brown on one side, turn gently over and brown the other side. Remove the cooked patties to a plate and continue until all the mixture is cooked. Combine all the sauce ingredients in a small, heavy-based pan and bring slowly to the boil, stirring continuously until thickened and cleared. Pour the sauce over the Egg Fu Yung to serve.

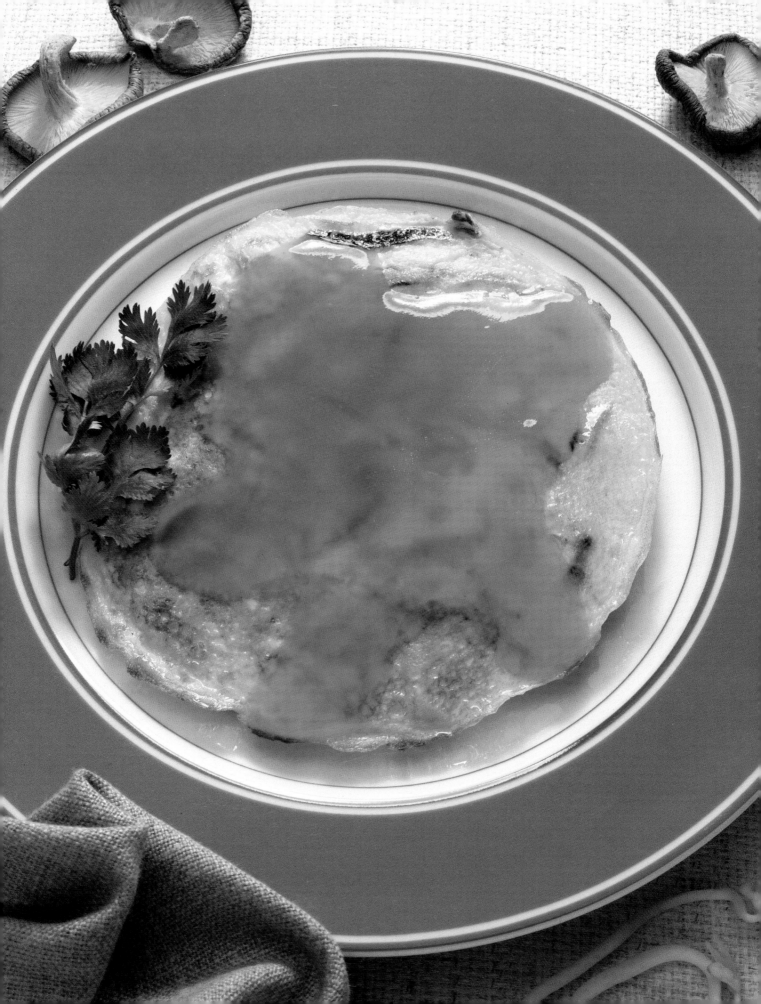

Shanghai Noodles

Preparation Time: 10 minutes **Cooking Time:** 6-8 minutes **Serves:** 4

In general, noodles are more popular in northern and eastern China, where wheat is grown, than in other parts of the country. Noodles make a popular snack in Chinese tea houses.

Ingredients

45ml/3 tbsps oil
120g/4oz chicken breast meat
120g/4oz Chinese cabbage
4 spring onions, thinly sliced

2 tbsps soy sauce
Freshly ground black pepper
Dash sesame oil
450g/1lb Shanghai noodles

Heat the oil in the wok and add the chicken cut into thin shreds. Stir-fry for 2-3 minutes. Meanwhile, cook the noodles in boiling salted water until just tender, about 6-8 minutes. Drain in a colander and rinse under hot water. Toss in the colander to drain and leave to dry.

Add the shredded Chinese cabbage and spring onions to the chicken in the wok along with the soy sauce, pepper and sesame oil. Cook about 1 minute and toss in the cooked noodles. Stir well and heat through. Serve immediately.

Top: colourful dancers entertain visitors in Middle Kingdom Park, Hong Kong.

Pork & Prawn Chow Mein

Preparation Time: 20 minutes **Cooking Time:** 12-14 minutes **Serves:** 4-6

Chinese chow mein dishes are usually based on noodles, using more expensive ingredients in small amounts. This makes economical everyday fare.

Ingredients

225g/8oz dried Chinese noodles
225g/8oz pork fillet, thinly sliced
1 carrot, peeled and shredded
1 small red pepper, cored, seeded
   and thinly sliced

90g/3oz bean sprouts
60g/2oz mange tout
1 tbsp rice wine or dry sherry
2 tbsps soy sauce
120g/4oz peeled, cooked prawns

Cook the noodles in plenty of boiling salted water for about 4-5 minutes. Rinse under hot water and drain thoroughly. Heat the wok and add oil. Stir-fry the pork 4-5 minutes or until almost cooked. Add the carrot to the wok and cook for 1-2 minutes. Core, seed and slice the red pepper and add with the remaining vegetables, wine and soy sauce. Cook for about 2 minutes. Add the cooked, drained noodles and prawns and toss over heat for 1-2 minutes. Serve immediately.

A farmer tends his geese in Nanning. Farmers work long and arduous hours, and many are lured to the cities in search of an easier life.

Aubergine & Pepper Szechuan Style

Preparation Time: 30 minutes **Cooking Time:** 7-8 minutes **Serves:** 4

Authentic Szechuan food is fiery hot. Outside China, restaurants often tone down the taste for Western palates.

Ingredients

1 large aubergine
2 cloves garlic, crushed
1 inch piece fresh ginger, shredded
1 onion, cut into 1-inch pieces
1 small green pepper, seeded,
  cored and cut into 1-inch pieces
1 small red pepper, seeded,
  cored and cut into 1-inch pieces
1 red or green chilli, seeded,
  cored and cut into thin strips

120ml/4fl oz chicken stock
1 tsp sugar
1 tsp vinegar
Pinch salt and pepper
1 tsp cornflour
1 tbsp soy sauce
Dash sesame oil
Oil for cooking

Cut the aubergine in half and score the surface. Sprinkle lightly with salt and leave to drain on paper towels for 30 minutes. After 30 minutes, squeeze the aubergine gently to extract any bitter juices and rinse thoroughly under cold water. Pat dry and cut the aubergine into 1-inch cubes. Heat about 3 tbsps oil in a wok. Add the aubergine and stir-fry for about 4-5 minutes. It may be necessary to add more oil as it cooks. Remove from the wok and set aside.

Reheat the wok and add 2 tbsps oil. Add the garlic and ginger and stir-fry for 1 minute. Add the onion and stir-fry for 2 minutes. Add the green pepper, red pepper and chilli pepper and stir-fry for 1 minute. Return the aubergine to the wok along with the remaining ingredients. Bring to the boil, stirring constantly, and cook until the sauce thickens and clears. Serve immediately.

Beef with Tomato & Pepper in Black Bean Sauce

Preparation Time: 25 minutes **Cooking Time:** 5 minutes **Serves:** 6

Black beans are a speciality of Cantonese cooking and give a pungent, salty taste to stir-fried dishes.

Ingredients

2 large tomatoes
2 tbsps water
2 tbsps salted black beans
60ml/4 tbsps dark soy sauce
1 tbsp cornflour
1 tbsp dry sherry
1 tsp sugar

450g/1lb rump steak, cut into strips
1 small green pepper, seeded
  and cored
60ml/4 tbsps oil
180ml/6 fl oz beef stock
Pinch pepper

Core tomatoes and cut them into 16 wedges. Crush the black beans, add the water and set aside. Combine soy sauce, cornflour, sherry, sugar and meat in a bowl and set aside. Cut pepper into ½-inch diagonal pieces. Heat the wok and add the oil. When hot, stir-fry the green pepper pieces for about 1 minute and remove.

Add the meat and the soy sauce mixture to the wok and stir-fry for about 2 minutes. Add the soaked black beans and the stock. Bring to the boil and allow to thicken slightly. Return the peppers to the wok and add the tomatoes and pepper. Heat through for 1 minute and serve immediately.

Top: Guilin is one of the most visited areas of China and although it benefits from tourism, farming is still the dominant economic force.

Quick Fried Prawns

Preparation Time: 30 minutes **Cooking Time:** 2 minutes **Serves:** 4-6

Prepared with either raw or cooked prawns, this is an incredibly delicious starter that is extremely easy to cook.

Ingredients

2lbs cooked prawns in their shells
2 cloves garlic, crushed
1 inch piece fresh ginger,
 finely chopped
1 tbsp chopped fresh coriander

3 tbsps oil
1 tbsp rice wine or dry sherry
1½ tbsps light soy sauce
Chopped spring onions to garnish

Shell the prawns except for the very tail ends. Place the prawns in a bowl with the remaining ingredients, except for the garnish, and leave to marinate for 30 minutes.

Heat the wok and add the prawns and the marinade. Stir-fry briefly to heat the prawns. Chop the onions roughly or cut into neat rounds. Sprinkle over the prawns to serve.

The bright lights of Hong Kong attract many Western visitors on their way to the more sedate pleasures of the Chinese mainland.

Sweet & Sour Pork

Preparation Time: 15 minutes **Cooking Time:** 15 minutes **Serves:** 2-4

This really needs no introduction because of its popularity. The dish originated in Canton, but is reproduced in most of the world's Chinese restaurants.

Ingredients

120g/4oz plain flour
60g/4 tbsps cornflour
1½ tsps baking powder
Pinch salt
1 tbsp oil
Water
225g/8oz pork fillet
1 onion, sliced
1 green pepper, seeded,
   cored and sliced
1 small can pineapple chunks,
   juice reserved
Oil for frying

Sweet and Sour Sauce
2 tbsps cornflour
120g/4oz light brown sugar
Pinch salt
120g/4 fl oz cider vinegar
1 tsp fresh ginger, grated
90ml/6 tbsps tomato ketchup
6 tbsps reserved pineapple juice

To prepare the batter, sift the flour, cornflour, baking powder and salt into a bowl. Make a well in the centre and add the oil and enough water to make a thick, smooth batter. Using a wooden spoon, stir the ingredients in the well, gradually incorporating flour from the outside, and beat until smooth.

Heat enough oil in a wok to deep-fry the pork. Cut the pork into 1/2-inch cubes, dip the cubes one at a time into the batter and drop into the hot oil. Fry 4-5 pieces of pork at a time and remove them with a draining spoon to paper towels. Continue until all the pork is fried. Pour off most of the oil from the wok and add the sliced onion, pepper and pineapple. Cook over high heat for 1-2 minutes. Remove and set aside.

Mix all the sauce ingredients together and pour into the wok. Bring slowly to the boil, stirring continuously until thickened. Allow to simmer for about 1-2 minutes or until completely clear. Add the vegetables, pineapple and pork cubes to the sauce and stir to coat completely. Reheat for 1-2 minutes and serve immediately.

Chicken Livers with Chinese Cabbage & Almonds

Preparation Time: 25 minutes **Cooking Time:** 4-5 minutes **Serves:** 4

Chicken livers need quick cooking, so they are a perfect choice for the Chinese stir-frying method.

Ingredients

225g/8oz chicken livers
45ml/3 tbsps oil
60g/2oz split blanched almonds
1 clove garlic, peeled
60g/2oz mange tout

8-10 Chinese cabbage leaves
2 tsps cornflour mixed with
   1 tbsp cold water
2 tbsps soy sauce
140ml/¼ pint chicken stock

Pick over the chicken livers and remove any discoloured areas or bits of fat. Cut the chicken livers into even-sized pieces. Heat a wok and pour in the oil. When the oil is hot, turn the heat down and add the almonds. Cook, stirring continuously, over gentle heat until the almonds are a nice golden brown. Remove and drain on paper towels. Add the garlic, cook for 1-2 minutes to flavour the oil and remove. Add the chicken livers and cook for about 2-3 minutes, stirring frequently. Remove the chicken livers and set them aside. Add the mange tout to the wok and stir-fry for 1 minute. Shred the Chinese cabbage leaves finely, add to the wok and cook for 1 minute. Remove the vegetables and set them aside.

   Mix together the cornflour and water with the soy sauce and stock. Pour into the wok and bring to the boil. Cook until thickened and clear. Return all the other ingredients to the sauce and reheat for 30 seconds. Serve immediately.

Top: rice paddies in Guangdong province. Paddies are still worked mainly by hand with a hoe and spade, or with an ox-drawn plough.

Peking Beef

Preparation Time: 25 minutes **Cooking Time:** 1½ hours **Serves:** 8

In China, meat is often simmered in large earthenware casseroles placed on asbestos mats. A wok is a convenient substitute and the stand does the work of the traditional mat.

Ingredients

900g/2lb joint of beef
430ml/¾ pint white wine
570ml/1 pint water
2 whole spring onions,
    roots trimmed
1-inch piece fresh ginger

3 star anise
140ml/¼ pint soy sauce
2 tsps sugar
1 carrot, peeled
2 sticks celery
½ mooli (daikon) radish, peeled

Place the beef in a wok and add the white wine, water, spring onions, ginger and anise. Cover and simmer for about 1 hour. Add the soy sauce and sugar, stir and simmer for 30 minutes longer, or until the beef is tender. Allow to cool in the liquid.

Shred the remaining vegetables finely. Blanch them in boiling water for about 1 minute. Rinse under cold water, drain and leave to dry.

When the meat is cold, remove it from the liquid and cut into thin slices. Arrange on a serving plate and strain the liquid over it. Scatter over the shredded vegetables and serve cold.

Selling tobacco at the market in Kweilin.

Mange Tout with Prawns

Preparation Time: 10 minutes **Cooking Time:** 6-8 minutes **Serves:** 2-4

Snow peas, pea pods and mange tout are all names for the same vegetable – bright green, crisp and edible, pods and all.

Ingredients

45ml/3 tbsps oil
60g/2oz split blanched almonds
120g/4oz mange tout
60g/2oz bamboo shoots, sliced
2 tsps cornflour

2 tsps light soy sauce
180ml/6 fl oz chicken stock
2 tbsps dry sherry
Salt and pepper
450g/1lb cooked, peeled prawns

Heat the oil in a wok. Add the almonds and cook over moderate heat until golden brown. Remove from the oil and drain on paper towels. To prepare the mange tout, tear off the stems and pull them downwards to remove any strings. If the mange tout are small, just remove the stalks. Add the mange tout to the hot oil and cook for about 1 minute. Remove and set aside with the almonds. Drain all the oil from the wok and mix together the cornflour and the remaining ingredients, except the prawns and bamboo shoots. Pour the mixture into the wok and stir constantly while bringing to the boil. Allow to simmer for 1-2 minutes until thickened and cleared. Stir in the prawns and all the other ingredients and heat through for about 1 minute. Serve immediately.

Top: a repair crew working on the Great Wall. Possibly the greatest man-made structure on earth, it stretches almost 6,000 kilometres across China.

Sweet-Sour Fish

Preparation Time: 25 minutes **Cooking Time:** 15-25 minutes **Serves:** 2

In China this dish is almost always prepared with freshwater fish, but sea bass is also an excellent choice.

Ingredients

1 sea bass, grey mullet or carp,
   weighing about 2lbs, cleaned
1 tbsp dry sherry
Few slices fresh ginger
120g/4oz sugar
90ml/6 tbsps cider vinegar
1 tbsp soy sauce

2 tbsps cornflour
1 clove garlic, crushed
2 spring onions, shredded
1 small carrot, peeled and
   finely shredded
30g/1oz bamboo shoots, shredded

Rinse the fish well inside and out. Make three diagonal cuts on each side of the fish with a sharp knife. Trim off the fins, leaving the dorsal fin on top. Trim the tail to two neat points. Bring enough water to cover the fish to the boil in a wok. Gently lower the fish into the boiling water and add the sherry and ginger. Cover the wok tightly and remove at once from the heat. Allow to stand 15-20 minutes to let the fish cook in the residual heat.

To test if the fish is cooked, pull the dorsal fin – if it comes off easily the fish is done. If not, return the wok to the heat and bring to the boil. Remove from the heat and leave the fish to stand a further 5 minutes. Transfer the fish to a heated serving dish and keep it warm. Take all but 4 tbsps of the fish cooking liquid from the wok. Add the remaining ingredients including the vegetables and cook, stirring constantly, until the sauce thickens. Spoon some of the sauce over the fish to serve and serve the rest separately.

Fishing on the Li River. The river flows slowly and is often shrouded in mists, lending a languid air to the landscape.

Beef with Broccoli

Preparation Time: 25 minutes **Cooking Time:** 4 minutes **Serves:** 2-3

The traditional Chinese method of cutting meat for stir-frying used in this recipe ensures that the meat will be tender and will cook quickly.

Ingredients

450g/1lb rump steak, partially frozen
60ml/4 tbsps dark soy sauce
1 tbsp cornflour
1 tbsp dry sherry
1 tsp sugar

225g/8oz fresh broccoli
90ml/6 tbsps oil
1 inch piece ginger, peeled
    and shredded
Salt and pepper

Trim any fat from the meat and cut into very thin strips across the grain. Strips should be about 3 inches long. Combine the meat with the soy sauce, cornflour, sherry and sugar. Stir well and leave long enough for the meat to completely defrost. Trim the florets from the stalks of the broccoli and cut them into even-sized pieces. Peel the stalks of the broccoli and cut into thin, diagonal slices. Slice the ginger into shreds. Heat a wok and add 2 tbsps of the oil to it. Add the broccoli and sprinkle with salt. Stir-fry, turning constantly, until the broccoli is dark green. Do not cook for longer than 2 minutes. Remove from the wok and set aside.

Place the remaining oil in the wok and add the ginger and beef. Stir-fry, turning constantly, for about 2 minutes. Return the broccoli to the pan and mix well. Heat through for 30 seconds and serve immediately.

Top: irrigating crops on a commune in Guilin, Guangxi province.

Kung Pao Prawns with Cashew Nuts

Preparation Time: 20 minutes **Cooking Time:** 3 minutes **Serves:** 6

It is said that Kung Pao invented this dish, but to this day no one knows who he was!

Ingredients

½ tsp chopped fresh ginger
1 tsp chopped garlic
1½ tbsps cornflour
¼ tsp bicarbonate of soda
Salt and pepper
¼ tsp sugar
450g/1lb uncooked prawns

60ml/4 tbsps oil
1 small onion, cut into dice
1 large or 2 small courgettes, cut into
  ½-inch cubes
1 small red pepper, cut into
  ½-inch cubes
60g/2oz cashew nuts

Sauce

180ml/6 fl oz chicken stock
1 tbsp cornflour
2 tsps chilli sauce

2 tsps bean paste (optional)
2 tsps sesame oil
1 tbsp dry sherry or rice wine

Mix together the ginger, garlic, 1½ tbsps cornflour, bicarbonate of soda, salt, pepper and sugar. If the prawns are unpeeled, remove the peels and the dark vein running along the rounded side. If large, cut in half, place in the dry ingredients and leave to stand for 20 minutes.

Heat the oil in a wok and when hot add the prawns. Cook, stirring over high heat for about 20 seconds, or just until the shrimp change colour. Transfer to a plate. Add the onion to the same oil in the wok and cook for about 1 minute. Add the courgettes and red pepper and cook about 30 seconds.

Mix the sauce ingredients together and add to the wok. Cook, stirring constantly, until the sauce is slightly thickened. Add the prawns and the cashew nuts and heat through completely.

Chicken with Cloud Ears

Preparation Time: 25 minutes **Cooking Time:** 5 minutes **Serves:** 6

Cloud ears is the delightful name for an edible tree fungus which is mushroom-like in taste and texture.

Ingredients

12 cloud ears, wood ears
   or other dried Chinese
   mushrooms, soaked in
   boiling water for 5 minutes
450g/1lb chicken breasts, boned and
   thinly sliced
1 egg white
2 tsps cornflour
2 tsps white wine

2 tsps sesame oil
280ml/½ pint oil
1 clove garlic
1 inch piece fresh ginger, left whole
280ml/½ pint chicken stock
1 tbsp cornflour
45ml/3 tbsps light soy sauce
Pinch salt and pepper

Soak the mushrooms until they soften and swell. Remove all the skin and bone from the chicken and cut it into thin slices. Mix the chicken with the egg white, cornflour, wine and sesame oil. Heat the wok for a few minutes and pour in the oil. Add the whole piece of ginger and whole garlic clove to the oil and cook for about 1 minute. Take them out and reduce the heat. Add about a quarter of the chicken at a time and stir-fry for about 1 minute. Remove and continue cooking until all the chicken is fried. Remove all but about 2 tbsps of the oil from the wok.

Drain the mushrooms and squeeze them to extract all the liquid. If using mushrooms with stems, remove the stems before slicing thinly. Cut cloud ears or wood ears into smaller pieces. Add to the wok and cook for about 1 minute. Add the stock and allow it to come almost to the boil. Mix together the cornflour and soy sauce and add a spoonful of the hot stock. Add the mixture to the wok, stirring constantly, and bring to the boil. Allow to boil 1-2 minutes or until thickened. The sauce will clear when the cornstarch has cooked sufficiently.

Return the chicken to the wok and add salt and pepper. Stir thoroughly for about 1 minute and serve immediately.

Singapore Fish

Preparation Time: 25 minutes **Cooking Time:** 10 minutes **Serves:** 6

The cuisine of Singapore was much influenced by that of China. In turn, the Chinese brought ingredients like curry powder into their own cuisine.

Ingredients

450g/1lb white fish fillets
1 egg white
1 tbsp cornflour
2 tsps white wine
Salt and pepper
Oil for frying
1 large onion, cut into ½-inch thick
    wedges
1 tbsp mild curry powder
1 small can pineapple pieces,
    drained and juice reserved, or
    ½ fresh pineapple, peeled
    and cubed

1 small can mandarin orange
    segments, drained and
    juice reserved
1 small can sliced water chestnuts,
    drained
1 tbsp cornflour mixed with juice
    of 1 lime
2 tsps sugar (optional)
Pinch salt and pepper

Starting at the tail end of the fillets, skin them using a sharp knife. Slide the knife back and forth along the length of each fillet, pushing the fish flesh along as you go. Cut the fish into even-sized pieces, about 2 inches square. Mix together the egg white, cornflour, wine, salt and pepper. Place the fish in the mixture and leave to stand while heating the oil.

When the oil is hot, fry a few pieces of fish at a time until light golden brown and crisp. Remove the fish to paper towels to drain, and continue until all the fish is cooked. Remove all but 1 tbsp of the oil from the wok and add the onion. Stir-fry the onion for 1-2 minutes and add the curry powder. Cook the onion and curry powder for a further 1-2 minutes. Add the juice from the pineapple and mandarin oranges and bring to the boil. Combine the cornflour and lime juice and add a spoonful of the boiling fruit juice. Return the mixture to the wok and cook until thickened, about 2 minutes. Taste and add sugar if desired. Add the fruit, water chestnuts and fried fish to the wok and stir to coat. Heat through for 1 minute and serve immediately.

Chicken with Walnuts & Celery

Preparation Time: 20 minutes **Cooking Time:** 8 minutes **Serves:** 4

Oyster sauce lends a subtle, slightly salty taste to this Cantonese dish.

Ingredients

225g/8oz boned chicken, cut into
    1-inch pieces
2 tsps soy sauce
2 tsps brandy
1 tsp cornflour
Salt and pepper
2 tbsps oil

1 clove garlic
120g/4oz walnut halves
3 sticks celery, cut in
    diagonal slices
2 tsps oyster sauce
140ml/¼ pint water or chicken stock

Combine the chicken with the soy sauce, brandy, cornflour, salt and pepper. Heat a wok and add the oil and garlic. Cook for about 1 minute to flavour the oil. Remove the garlic and add the chicken in two batches. Stir-fry quickly without allowing the chicken to brown. Remove the chicken and add the walnuts to the wok. Cook for about 2 minutes until the walnuts are slightly brown and crisp. Slice the celery, add to the wok and cook for about 1 minute. Add the oyster sauce and water and bring to the boil. When boiling, return the chicken to the pan and stir to coat all the ingredients well. Serve immediately.

In China many crops are still harvested by hand and this back-breaking task is one that has to be endured by almost all members of the family.

Szechuan Fish

Preparation Time: 30 minutes **Cooking Time:** 10 minutes **Serves:** 6

The piquant spiciness of Szechuan pepper is quite different from that of black or white pepper. Beware, though, too much can numb the mouth temporarily!

Ingredients

Chilli peppers for garnish
450g/1lb white fish fillets
Pinch salt and pepper
1 egg
75g/5 tbsps flour
90ml/6 tbsps white wine
Oil for frying
60g/2oz cooked ham, diced
1-inch piece fresh ginger, finely diced
½-1 red or green chilli pepper,
    cored, seeded and finely diced

6 water chestnuts, finely diced
4 spring onions, finely chopped
45ml/3 tbsps light soy sauce
1 tsp cider vinegar or rice wine vinegar
½ tsp ground Szechuan
    pepper (optional)
280ml/½ pint light stock
1 tbsp cornflour dissolved with
    2 tbsps water
2 tsps sugar

To prepare the garnish, choose unblemished chilli peppers with the stems on. Using a small, sharp knife, cut the peppers in strips, starting from the pointed end. Cut down to within ½ inch of the stem end. Rinse out the seeds under cold running water and place the peppers in iced water. Leave the peppers to soak for at least 4 hours or overnight until they open up like flowers.

Cut the fish fillets into 2-inch pieces and season with salt and pepper. Beat the egg well and add flour and wine to make a batter. Dredge the fish lightly with flour and then dip into the batter. Mix the fish well.

Heat a wok and when hot, add enough oil to deep-fry the fish. When the oil is hot, fry a few pieces of fish at a time, until golden brown. Drain and proceed until all the fish is cooked. Remove all but 1 tbsp of oil from the wok and add the ham, ginger, diced chilli pepper, water chestnuts and spring onions. Cook for about 1 minute and add the soy sauce and vinegar. If using Szechuan pepper, add at this point. Stir well and cook for a further 1 minute. Remove the vegetables from the pan and set them aside. Add the stock to the wok and bring to the boil. When boiling, add 1 spoonful of the hot stock to the cornflour mixture. Add the mixture back to the stock and reboil, stirring constantly until thickened. Stir in the sugar and return the fish and vegetables to the sauce. Heat through for 30 seconds and serve immediately.

Almond Float with Fruit

Preparation Time: 25 minutes   **Serves:** 6-8

Sweet dishes are not often served in the course of a Chinese meal. Banquets are the exception, and this elegant fruit salad is certainly special enough.

Ingredients

1 envelope unflavored gelatine
90ml/6 tbsps cold water
90g/3oz sugar
280ml/½ pint milk
1 tsp almond essence
Few drops red or yellow food
   colouring (optional)

Almond Sugar Syrup
90g/3oz sugar
570ml/1 pint water
½ tsp almond extract
Fresh fruit such as kiwi, mango,
   pineapple, bananas, lychees,
   oranges or satsumas, peaches,
   berries, cherries, grapes or starfruit
Fresh mint for garnish

Allow the gelatine to soften in the cold water for about 10 minutes or until spongy. Put in a large mixing bowl. Bring 180ml/6 fl oz water to the boil and stir in the sugar. Pour into the gelatine and water mixture and stir until gelatine and sugar dissolves. Add milk, flavouring, and food colouring if using. Mix well and pour into a 8-inch square tin. Chill in the refrigerator until set (2 hours).

Mix the sugar and water for the syrup together in a heavy-based pan. Cook over gentle heat until the sugar dissolves. Bring to the boil and allow to boil for about 2 minutes, or until the syrup thickens slightly. Add the almond extract and allow to cool at room temperature. Chill in the refrigerator until ready to use.

Prepare the fruit and place in an attractive serving dish. Pour over the chilled syrup and mix well. Cut the set almond float into 1-inch diamond shapes or cubes. Use a spatula to remove them from the pan and stir them gently into the fruit mixture. Decorate with sprigs of fresh mint to serve.

Top: the Temple of Heaven in Peking marks a sacred spot where emperors used to pray for a good harvest.

Sweet Bean Wontons

Preparation Time: 15-20 minutes   **Serves:** 6

Wonton snacks, either sweet or savoury, are another popular tea house treat. Made from prepared wonton wrappers and ready-made bean paste, these couldn't be more simple.

Ingredients

15 wonton wrappers
225g/8oz sweet red bean paste
1 tbsp cornflour
60ml/4 tbsps cold water
Oil for deep frying
Honey

Take a wonton wrapper in the palm of your hand and place a little of the red bean paste slightly above the centre. Mix together the cornstarch and water and moisten the edge around the filling. Fold over, slightly off centre. Pull the sides together, using the cornflour and water paste to stick the two together. Turn inside out by gently pushing the filled centre. Heat enough oil in a wok for deep-fat frying and when hot, put in 4 of the filled wontons at a time. Cook until crisp and golden and remove to paper towels to drain. Repeat with the remaining filled wontons. Serve drizzled with honey.

A magazine vendor smiles proudly for the camera.

Spun Fruits

Preparation Time: 25 minutes **Cooking Time:** 10-15 minutes **Serves:** 4

Often called toffee fruits, this sweet consists of fruit fried in batter and coated with a thin, crisp caramel glaze.

Ingredients

Batter
120g/4oz flour, sifted
Pinch salt
1 egg

140ml/¼ pint water and milk mixed
    half and half
Oil for deep frying

Caramel Syrup
225g/8oz sugar
45ml/3 tbsps water
1 tbsp oil

1 banana, peeled and cut into
    1-inch pieces
Ice water
1 large apple, peeled, cored and cut
    into 1-inch chunks

To prepare the batter, combine all the batter ingredients, except the oil for deep frying, in a liquidiser or food processor and process to blend. Pour into a bowl and dip in the prepared fruit.

In a heavy-based saucepan, combine the sugar with the water and oil and cook over very low heat until the sugar dissolves. Bring to the boil and allow to cook rapidly until a pale caramel colour. While the sugar is dissolving, heat the oil in a wok and fry the batter-dipped fruit, a few pieces at a time. While the fruit is still hot and crisp, use chopsticks or a pair of tongs to dip the fruit into the hot caramel syrup. Stir each piece around to coat evenly. Dip immediately into ice water to harden the syrup and place each piece on a greased dish. Continue cooking all the fruit in the same way. Once the caramel has hardened and the fruit has cooled, transfer to a clean serving plate.

Almond Cookies

Preparation Time: 10 minutes **Cooking Time:** 12-15 minutes per batch **Makes:** 30

In China these are often eaten as a between-meal snack. In Western-style cuisine, they make a good accompaniment to fruit or sorbet.

Ingredients

1 stick butter or margarine
60g/4 tbsps granulated sugar
2 tbsps light brown sugar
1 egg, beaten
Almond essence
120g/4oz plain flour

1 tsp baking powder
Pinch salt
30g/1oz ground almonds,
    blanched or unblanched
2 tbsps water
30 whole blanched almonds

Cream the butter or margarine together with the two sugars until light and fluffy. Divide the beaten egg in half and add half to the sugar mixture with a few drops of the almond essence and beat until smooth. Reserve the remaining egg for later use. Sift the flour, baking powder and salt into the egg mixture and add the ground almonds. Stir well by hand. Shape the mixture into small balls and place well apart on a lightly greased baking sheet. Flatten slightly and press an almond on to the top of each one.

Mix the reserved egg with the water and brush each cookie before baking. Place in a preheated 180°C/350°F/Gas Mark 4 oven and bake for 12-15 minutes. Cookies will be a pale golden colour when done.

Top: the province of Yunnan is poor and sparsely populated, but its warm climate and high rainfall make it perfect for agriculture.

Almond Cookies 68
Almond Float with Fruit 62
Aubergine and Pepper Szechuan Style 34
Barbecued Spare Ribs 12
Beef with Broccoli 50
Beef with Tomato and Pepper in Black Bean
    Sauce 36
Cantonese Egg Fu Yung 28
Chicken Livers with Chinese Cabbage and
    Almonds 42
Chicken with Cloud Ears 54
Chicken with Walnuts and Celery 58
Crab and Sweetcorn Soup 18
Desserts:
    Almond Cookies 68
    Almond Float with Fruit 62
    Spun Fruits 66
    Sweet Bean Wontons 64
Fried Rice 26
Fish and Seafood:
    Kung Pao Prawns with Cashew
        Nuts 52
    Mange Tout with Prawns 46
    Quick Fried Prawns 38
    Singapore Fish 56
    Sweet and Sour Fish 48
    Szechuan Fish 60
Hot and Sour Soup 14
Kung Pao Prawns with Cashew
    Nuts 52
Meat Dishes:
    Beef with Broccoli 50
    Beef with Tomato and Pepper in Black
        Bean Sauce 36
    Peking Beef 44
    Pork and Prawn Chow Mein 32
    Sweet and Sour Pork 40

Mange Tout with Prawns 46
Peking Beef 44
Pork and Prawn Chow Mein 32
Pot Sticker Dumplings 22
Poultry:
    Chicken Livers with Chinese Cabbage
        and Almonds 42
    Chicken with Cloud Ears 54
    Chicken with Walnuts and Celery 58
Quick Fried Prawns 38
Sesame Chicken Wings 16
Shanghai Noodles 30
Side Dishes:
    Aubergine and Pepper Szechuan
        Style 34
    Cantonese Egg Fu Yung 28
    Fried Rice 26
    Shanghai Noodles 30
    Special Mixed Vegetables 24
Singapore Fish 56
Soups:
    Crab and Sweetcorn Soup 18
    Hot and Sour Soup 14
    Wonton Soup 10
Special Mixed Vegetables 24
Spring Rolls 20
Spun Fruits 66
Starters:
    Barbequed Spare Ribs 12
    Pot Sticker Dumplings 22
    Sesame Chicken Wings 16
    Spring Rolls 20
Sweet and Sour Fish 48
Sweet and Sour Pork 40
Sweet Bean Wontons 64
Szechuan Fish 60
Wonton Soup 10